D1093835

ANCIENT
CIVILIZATIONS

VOLUME 8

PHOENICIANS — SOCIAL ORGANIZATION

GROLIER
EDUCATIONAL

Published 2000 by Grolier Educational
Sherman Turnpike
Danbury, Connecticut 06816

Reprinted in 2001

© 2000 Brown Partworks Limited

Set ISBN: 0-7172-9471-4
Volume ISBN: 0-7172-9479-X

Library of Congress Cataloging-in-Publication Data
Ancient civilizations.
  p. cm.— Includes bibliographical references and indexes.
Summary: A multi-volume encyclopedia with alphabetically
arranged topics relating to ancient civilizations and the
discovery of famous archaeological sites.
ISBN 0-7172-9471-4 (set: alk. paper). — ISBN 0-7172-9472-2
(v. 1: alk. paper). — ISBN 0-7172-9473-0 (v. 2: alk. paper). —
ISBN 0-7172-9474-9 (v. 3: alk. paper).
1. Civilization. Ancient Encyclopedias, Juvenile. 2. Prehistoric
peoples Encyclopedias, Juvenile. 3. Antiquities Encyclopedias,
Juvenile. 4. Excavations (Archaeology) Encyclopedias, Juvenile.
[1. Civilization, Ancient Encyclopedias. 2. Prehistoric peoples
Encyclopedias. 3. Antiquities Encyclopedias. 4. Excavations
(Archaeology) Encyclopedias. 5. Archaeology Encyclopedias.]
I. Grolier Educational (Firm)
CB311.A5197 2000   99-18387
930—dc21   CIP

For information address the publisher:
Grolier Educational, Sherman Turnpike,
Danbury, Connecticut 06816

FOR BROWN PARTWORKS LTD

Project editor: Shona Grimbly
Design: Wilson Design Associates
Picture research: Veneta Bullen
Text editors: Chris King
                       Sally MacEachern
Managing editor: Lindsey Lowe
Consultant: Paul Bahn

Printed in Singapore

Maps

The maps in this book show you the locations of cities and sites of the
distant past. Ancient cities and sites are shown by red dots, while
modern-day cities and sites are shown by black dots.

Ancient place names and names of countries are shown in bold type,
while modern place and country names are shown in ordinary type.

About this book

This is one of a set of 10 books telling the stories of the
peoples and civilizations of the distant past. Thousands
of years ago hunter-gathering peoples began to settle
down in villages and start to farm. They also began to
develop many remarkable skills. They learned to make
clay into bricks and pots, they learned to mine metals
and fashion them into ornaments, tools, and weapons,
and they learned how to weave cloth out of the fibers
of plants. In a surprisingly short time some of these
peoples were living in large cities and were trading
with other people great distances away.

   The books in this set relate these achievements and
also describe some of the notable inventions that
helped human beings along the road to civilization,
such as the wheel, the compass—and sanitation. Some
of the entries in this book describe a particular
people or civilization in depth, while other entries take
a subject, such as "Numbers and Counting," and
examine it across a range of civilizations. Other entries
look at archaeological sites of special interest and tell
the story of their discovery. The entries are arranged
alphabetically and are illustrated with photographs,
drawings, and maps. Each entry ends with a list of
cross-references to other entries in the set. At the end
of the book there is an illustrated timeline to help you
relate the civilizations to each other in time. There is
also a useful "Further Reading" list and an index
covering the whole set.

Picture credits:
Cover E T Archive/Hittite Museum, Ankara; title page AKG/Hilbich,
AKG/Erich Lessing 4; E T Archives/Archaeological Museum, Cagliari 5;
Mary Evans Picture Library 6t; AKG/Erich Lessing 7 & 8; Werner Forman
Archive 9; Tony Stone Associates 10 & 11t; South American Pictures/David
Horwell 12; Werner Forman Archive 13 & 14; AKG 15t; E T Archive 15b;
AKG 16b; Sonia Halliday 18; Werner Forman Archive/Art & History
Museum, Shanghai 19; E T Archive/Hittite Museum, Ankara 20; AKG/
Erich Lessing 21; AKG 22; E T Archive/Devizes Museum 23; South
American Pictures/Chris Sharp 24; Eye Ubiquitous/James Davis 25; E T
Archive/British Museum 26; Corbis/Aisa/Egyptian Museum 27; E T
Archive 28-30; Corbis/Gianni Dagli Orti/Archaeological Museum, Greece
31; Mary Evans Picture Library 32; Werner Forman Archive/National
Museum, Copenhagen 33; AKG/Erich Lessing 34; Sonia Halliday/FHC
Birch 35; E T Archive 36; AKG 37; E T Archive/Natural History Museum,
Bucharest 38; AKG/Hilbich 39 and 41; Travel Ink/Ronald Budkin 42; Eye
Ubiquitous/Paul Seheult 44; Sonia Halliday 45; Portfolio Pictures 46;
Corbis/Yannan Arthus-Bertrand 47; South American Pictures/Tony Morris
48; Ancient Art & Architecture 49b; Werner Forman Archives/National
Museum, Dares Salam 51; Werner Forman Archive/Private Collection 52;
E T Archive 53; Eye Ubiquitous/ John Miles 54; AKG/Erich Lessing 55;
Corbis/Francesc Murstada 56t; Werner Forman Archive/British Museum
56b; Werner Forman Archive/ Viking Ship Museum, Bygdoy 57; E T
Archive/Bibliotheque Nationale, Paris 60; Werner Forman Archive 61;
Erich Lessing/National Museum of Archaeology 62; Portfolio Pictures 63;
AKG/Erich Lessing 64; Werner Forman/Dr E Stroudhal 65;
Corbis/Aisa/National Library, Paris 66; AKG 67.

Maps: Colin Woodman. Artworks: Mark Topham 40 and 58; Salamander
Picture Library 49; Colin Woodman 50.
Quotation in "Voice from the Past" on page 17 from Peter Mantin, *The
Roman World*, Cambridge University Press, 1992.

CONTENTS

VOLUME EIGHT

PHOENICIANS

The Phoenicians were a nation of great seafarers and traders from the shores of the eastern Mediterranean Sea. No one knows where they came from originally, but they probably arrived in the Mediterranean region about 3000 B.C. Their homeland there was a narrow coastal strip now divided among Syria, Lebanon, and Israel. The Phoenicians were renowned as merchants, navigators, skilled boatbuilders, and gifted craftsmen. They were also famous for their learning, inventing an alphabet that was adopted by the Greeks and later formed the basis of all the alphabets used in the West today.

The name Phoenicia comes from the Greek *phoinix*, meaning red-purple. The Greeks called the Phoenicians *Phoinikes* (the red-purple men) because of their most important product, a purple dye that was used to stain cloth. The Phoenicians called themselves Canaanites and were descended from the Bronze Age people of Canaan (ancient Syria and Palestine). Canaan also means "land of purple" in the Semitic language.

THE CANAANITES
During the early Bronze Age (3000–2000 B.C.) the Canaanites built a number of great cities, including the ports of Byblos and Ugarit, which became important trading centers between 2000 and 1500 B.C. However,

▲ *The ruins of the city of Byblos as they are today. On the coast of the Mediterranean Sea, Byblos was the Phoenicians' main port for the export of cedarwood. It remained a great trading center well into Roman times.*

after 1550 B.C. the cities of Canaan were conquered and ruled by a series of foreign powers, including the Hittites, Egyptians, and Mycenaeans.

The history of Phoenicia really begins around 1100 B.C., when the Phoenicians seized an opportunity to gain their freedom. At this time the civilizations of southern Europe and western Asia were threatened by invading tribes called the Sea Peoples. These fierce warriors attacked the Egyptians, conquered the Hittites, and contributed to the downfall of the Mycenaeans in Greece. The Mycenaeans had dominated sea trade in the Mediterranean since the 1600s. The weakening of all these nations gave the Phoenicians the chance not only to reclaim their independence but also to win control of sea trade in the region.

PHOENICIAN INFLUENCE

Over the next 250 years Phoenician power and influence spread throughout the Mediterranean region. Their cities set up trading stations, then colonies, in Cyprus and western Sicily, and at Gades (modern Cadiz) in Spain. Carthage, a port on the north coast of Africa, was another important colony. It was founded in 814 B.C. by the city of Tyre. Tyre and Sidon, in particular, grew into wealthy cities and centers of learning. Built on two offshore islands, Tyre was especially powerful because it was very difficult to attack. Nebuchadnezzar,

king of Babylon, laid siege to it without success for 13 years during the 500s B.C.

During the 900s B.C. the king of Tyre made an alliance with the Hebrews under King David and his successor, Solomon. According to the Bible King Hiram of Tyre provided

▲ *This pottery funerary mask was found in Sardinia, which was one of Phoenicia's trading colonies.*

ROYAL PURPLE

Phoenician purple cloth was in demand throughout the Mediterranean region because purple was the color worn by kings. To make the purple dye, shells of murex snails (found in the sea) were cracked, and the soft creatures inside removed. Their rotting bodies yielded a yellow liquid that darkened to purple when boiled and processed.

Tyre and Sidon were notorious for the stench given off by the rotting snails. Each snail produced only a tiny drop of liquid, so up to 60,000 mollusks were needed to make 1 lb. (450g) of dye. Skilled dyers could produce a range of colors, from pale pink to deep purple. Tailors then fashioned some of the cloth into ready-made robes.

cedarwood and craftsmen experienced in working "gold and silver, iron, stone, and wood, as well as purple, violet, and crimson yarn and fine linen," to help build Solomon's temple. Hiram sent shipbuilders to establish a Hebrew fleet on the Red Sea. From there Solomon's ships, manned by Phoenician sailors, went out on trading missions. Once every three years, the Bible tells us, "this fleet of merchantmen came home, bringing gold and silver, ivory, apes, and monkeys."

EXPLORATION

By about 850 B.C. the Phoenicians had colonized the Mediterranean islands of Corsica, Sardinia, Malta, and Gozo, and possibly also parts of the Greek mainland. They controlled the Strait of Gibraltar, where the Mediterranean Sea narrows to a distance of 8 miles (13km) as its waters mingle with the vast Atlantic Ocean. Daring Phoenician sailors ventured beyond this strait to visit the Azores and possibly Cornwall on the southwest tip of England, a center for tin mining. Later, during the 600s B.C. Phoenician seamen led an Egyptian expedition that sailed all the

way around the African coast, a voyage that lasted three years according to the Greek historian Herodotus.

The development of Phoenicia was influenced by its geography. To the west the waters of the Mediterranean Sea formed a natural boundary. To the east the mountains of Lebanon made another protective barrier between Phoenicia and its powerful neighbors inland. The great cities of Phoenicia —Tyre, Sidon, Byblos, Berytus (Beirut),

▲ *An artist's impression of a Phoenician trading ship. It had a wide hull to hold plenty of cargo.*

▼ *The extent of the Phoenician trading empire.*

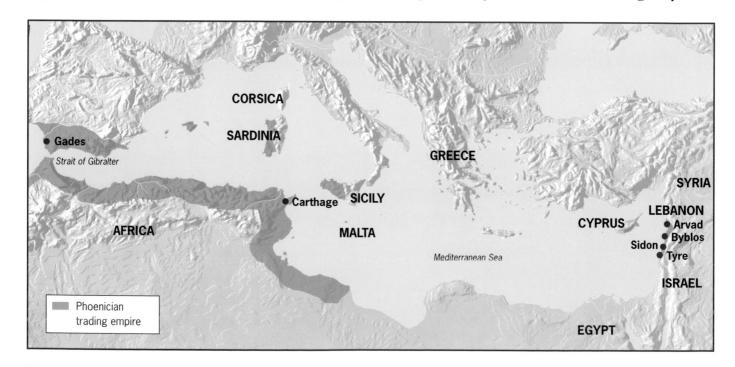

CORSICA

SARDINIA

• Gades

Strait of Gibralter

GREECE

• Carthage SICILY

AFRICA MALTA

CYPRUS

SYRIA

LEBANON
• Arvad
• Byblos

Sidon •
• Tyre

ISRAEL

Mediterranean Sea

EGYPT

■ Phoenician trading empire

and Arvad—began as small sea ports that grew rich on trading profits. But miles of rugged coastline separated these settlements and prevented Phoenicia from becoming a unified kingdom. Instead, it flourished as a chain of powerful city-states.

Although small, Phoenicia held rich resources. Cloth and timber formed the basis of Phoenician trade. The shallow waters offshore were a rich fishing ground and the source of the murex snails that produced the famous purple dye. Inland the coastal strip was well watered by streams and rivers. In this fertile soil farmers grew wheat, barley, grapes, and olives, and pastured their herds. But Phoenicia's greatest

A NEW ALPHABET

The Phoenicians spoke a Semitic language related to Hebrew and Babylonian. From the Babylonians they also learned cuneiform writing, a script of wedge-shaped symbols. Around 1200 B.C. they developed their own alphabet of 22 letters (all consonants). It was an immense improvement since the cuneiform scripts in use at this time could have as many as 600 different symbols. Later the Greeks adapted the Phoenician alphabet, adding vowels. From them the alphabet passed to the Romans, and through the Romans it became the basis of all Western alphabets. Some Phoenician words still survive in English and other European languages. The English words "bible" and "bibliography" (a book list), for example, are derived from the name Byblos, the Phoenician port famous for its trade in papyrus, the writing material of the ancient world.

◄ *This elegant glass container for perfume or ointment was made by Phoenician craftsmen in the fifth century B.C. using the sand-core method. They poured layers of molten glass over a shaped sand mold, and when the glass coating set, the sand was emptied out. Colored glass was then dripped onto the vessel, which was rolled on a flat surface before the glass cooled.*

asset lay in the mountains—the mighty forests that grew on the steep hillsides. The cedars of Lebanon were prized for their hard, long-lasting timber. The Phoenicians used the wood for their own shipbuilding and also sold large quantities for export.

TRADE GOODS

Phoenician merchants sold agricultural produce such as grain, oil, wine, and raisins. They also acted as middlemen, selling crops and goods produced by other peoples. Traders imported metals and other raw materials from around the Mediterranean for Phoenician craftsmen to make into beautiful objects. Smiths cast and hammered gold, silver, and bronze into tools, weapons, and jewelry. Ivory brought from Africa was carved into delicate panels to decorate chairs, beds, and chests. Glassworkers made glass from silica-rich sand and wood ash. They shaped molten glass around a sand or clay mold and allowed it to set before destroying the mold. Later Phoenicians may have invented glassblowing.

The Phoenicians shared some of their gods and goddesses with other

ancient civilizations, including Egypt and Babylon. They worshiped the Egyptian sun god Re and the goddess Hathor, and the Mesopotamian god of storms, Hadad. The Phoenicians usually called their deities simply Baal (lord) or Baalat (lady). On altars called *tophets* they offered animal sacrifices. Some historians believe that they may also have sacrificed young children.

In 842 B.C. Phoenicia was conquered by the Assyrian Empire. For 200 years Phoenician cities suffered under harsh Assyrian rule. During the 600s B.C. they passed first into the hands of the Babylonians, then the Persians. The Persians allowed the civilizations they conquered many freedoms, so the cities prospered again, especially Sidon. The Phoenician fleet fought for the Persians

in their wars against the Greeks, only to be destroyed by the Greek navy at the Battle of Salamis in 480 B.C.

In 330 B.C. Phoenicia was conquered again, this time by Alexander the Great of Macedonia. Under his successors Phoenicia thrived as a center of culture and commerce until 64 B.C., when it became part of the Roman Empire and ceased to have a separate identity.

SEE ALSO:

◆ ASSYRIANS
◆ EXPLORATION
◆ NAVIGATION
◆ PERSIAN EMPIRE
◆ SHIPS

▲ *A sacrificial altar in the city of Carthage. The Phoenicians used altars like this to sacrifice small animals. Some historians believe that parents may also have sacrificed their first-born child to the gods, although the extent of this practice may have been exaggerated.*

POLYNESIANS

◀ These carved wooden statues are found at a temple site on the west coast of Hawaii and depict traditional Polynesian gods. The Hawaiian islands form the northernmost point of Polynesia and were settled sometime around 400 A.D.

The Pacific Ocean covers a third of the earth's surface. The settlement of the remote and widely separated islands of this vast expanse of water was the major achievement of the people we now call **Polynesians**. In modern times the Polynesians are scattered over an area that forms an immense triangle, with the Hawaiian Islands, New Zealand, and Easter Island forming its corners. Although they are spread over such a large area, genetically the Polynesians form a single group. They speak dialects of the same language, and many features of their culture are similar.

The exact origins of the Polynesians are uncertain. Expansion of human settlement into the remote Pacific began in about 1600 B.C. with the appearance of a distinctive culture called Lapita. This is shown by the pottery found at Lapita sites, which is usually elaborately decorated with stamped designs. There are many of these sites spread over Melanesia and

AMAZING VOYAGES

The achievement of the Polynesians in settling the remote islands of the Pacific is all the more impressive when we realize that it was achieved without navigation instruments or charts. Polynesian double-hulled canoes were large and fast, and were capable of voyaging thousands of miles. The canoes were sailed by skilled navigators who used their detailed knowledge of the stars, cloud patterns, winds and swells, and the habits of seabirds to keep track of their position and locate land. In 1976 the skill of these navigators was demonstrated when the *Hokulea*, a replica of a traditional Polynesian canoe, was sailed from Tahiti to Hawaii using age-old navigation techniques.

western Polynesia from New Guinea to Samoa. Some archaeologists believe that the Lapita culture originated in Southeast Asia, while others think that it developed locally in Melanesia. It is generally agreed, however, that the Lapita people were the ancestors of the Polynesians.

The Lapita way of life seems to have been very much focused on the sea. Most Lapita sites are coastal villages, and in some cases people even seem to have built their houses on pillars over

The Lapita peoples were highly skilled navigators and boatbuilders

the water. The sea provided a good deal of food—fish and shellfish—and shell was used to make fishhooks and adzes (axes) as well as ornaments, such as armbands, beads, and other decorative and valuable objects. The Lapita colonists also brought domestic animals and plants with them to the islands they settled.

The expansion of the Lapita people seems to have been rapid. They must have had sophisticated boatbuilding and navigation techniques. It is likely that the development of the large double-hulled sailing canoe was a key factor in their success. The Lapita

▼ *A modern-day Polynesian boatbuilder using traditional techniques to make a canoe.*

migrations must have been deliberate, since they carried with them sufficient equipment, plants, and animals, as well as enough people, to establish successful settlements. Their voyages were certainly not one-way; there is evidence of long-distance trading networks for obsidian (volcanic glass) and other items linking Lapita communities. The Lapita culture seems to have lasted for about 1,000 years.

COLONIZING THE PACIFIC

The main features of Polynesian culture seem to have developed on the islands of Samoa and Tonga. Like their Lapita ancestors, the Polynesians were seafarers. About 300 B.C. voyagers from Samoa and Tonga began another eastward migration. They discovered and settled the Cook Islands, Tahiti, the Tuamotus, and the Marquesas Islands. By 400 A.D. both Hawaii and Easter Island—two points of the Polynesian triangle—had been colonized. New Zealand—the third point of the triangle, and the hardest to reach, was settled about 1000 A.D.

There is no doubt that the Polynesian colonizing voyages were deliberate and that exploration to find new islands preceded colonization.

▲ *Polynesian villagers with their traditional thatched huts.*

▼ *The so-called Polynesian triangle, formed by Hawaii, New Zealand, and Easter Island.*

Like their Lapita ancestors, they took with them everything necessary to establish successful settlements. In a few cases the colonies were not successful and were abandoned.

Polynesian societies were organized into tribes and clans. Normally they were further divided into chiefs and commoners, and there was also a form of slavery. The most elaborate social hierarchies developed in Hawaii,

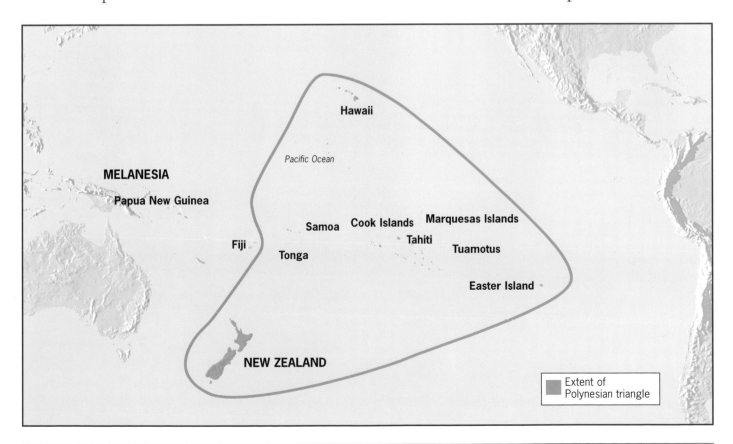

Pacific Ocean

Hawaii

MELANESIA

Papua New Guinea

Fiji

Tonga

Samoa

Cook Islands

Tahiti

Marquesas Islands

Tuamotus

Easter Island

NEW ZEALAND

Extent of Polynesian triangle

EASTER ISLAND

One of the most amazing feats of the Polynesian navigators was to reach and colonize Rapa Nui, or Easter Island. This tiny speck of land, only 64 square miles (166 sq. km) in area, is one of the most remote of the Polynesian islands. The difficulty of the voyage probably means that it was settled only once some time in the early centuries A.D. The people then developed in isolation, building great stone platforms (*ahu*) all around the shoreline and carving hundreds of huge stone statues (*moai*) of their ancestors, many of which were placed on these platforms, facing away from the sea.

It seems that the islanders brought about their own downfall by destroying the forests of huge palm trees that covered the island, even though the trees were the foundation of their society. The resulting lack of timber stopped the production of statues, since there were no more rollers, levers, or rope. The inhabitants were also no longer able to build canoes, which meant that no more deep-sea fish could be caught. There was no more fuel for cremations, and burial became the new method of disposing of the dead. Food became scarce, and violence erupted after centuries of peace. Villages and clans raided each other, toppling their rivals' statues.

The ancestor worship of the past was replaced by a new social system based on a warrior elite. Every year a new leader, or "Birdman," was elected by means of an endurance race. Each candidate's representative had to go down a cliff, swim out to an islet, and bring back intact the first egg of the sooty tern. By the time the first Europeans arrived on Easter Sunday 1722, the population had declined catastrophically, and there were virtually no trees left on the island.

▲ *These stone statues (or* moai*) are found at Ahu Nau Nau, where the original inhabitants of Easter Island first landed. Over 800 such statues are found on the island.*

▲ *A stonewalled ceremonial enclosure on Tahiti. Such enclosures were used for meetings and religious rituals and are found throughout Polynesia. The British explorer James Cook saw human sacrifices being made here during his stay in 1769.*

Tonga, and Tahiti. The Polynesians shared a broadly similar set of religious beliefs. Ceremonial enclosures, known as *marae*, were a prominent feature of settlements and provided a focus for ceremonies and community meetings.

FARMING TECHNIQUES

Polynesian agriculture was based on a range of crops, including yams, sweet potato, taro, breadfruit, bananas, and sugarcane. The Polynesians practiced shifting cultivation, which meant that a patch of land was cleared, the vegetation was burned, and then crops were planted. Later, the plot was allowed to lie fallow (unplanted) and gradually return to natural vegetation.

On some islands very complex systems of irrigation were used to bring water to crops. Taro, in particular, was grown in irrigated fields. Pigs, dogs, and chickens were the main domestic animals, although not all of them were

introduced to all islands. Most domesticated plants used by the settlers originated in Southeast Asia. The sweet potato, however, came from the Americas, which indicates that at some point, the Polynesians reached South America and brought it back.

Over time the tradition of making pottery, which the Polynesians had inherited from the Lapita culture, seems to have declined, and complex decoration was simplified or abandoned completely. Finally, the Polynesians seem to have stopped making pottery entirely.

SEE ALSO:

◆ **ABORIGINES OF AUSTRALIA**
◆ **EXPLORATION**
◆ **MAORIS**
◆ **NAVIGATION**

POMPEII

Pompeii was a city in southern Italy that flourished during the Roman Empire. In 79 A.D. a nearby volcano erupted and buried the city in lava and ash, preserving it for the next 2,000 years. It was rediscovered in the 18th century and is now one of the most famous archaeological sites in the world. Millions of people from all over the world have visited the excavations to see for themselves how people lived in ancient Roman times.

Pompeii was just an ordinary city of no particular importance. It became a Roman community in 91 B.C., and over the next 150 years many wealthy Romans built houses there, enjoying its beautiful climate on the shores of the Mediterranean Sea. There was one drawback to the city's location: it was overlooked by the volcano of Mount Vesuvius. However, this didn't bother its citizens, who had never known a volcanic eruption. In 62 A.D. Vesuvius rumbled, and Pompeii was shaken and damaged by a severe earthquake.

▲ *The ruins of Pompeii as they are today. It was a walled city with long straight roads leading to seven gates. This view from the north wall shows the central paved street, which leads toward the forum.*

◄ *A veiw of the forum at Pompeii, looking through one of the gates, with the peak of Mount Vesuvius in the background.*

▼ *This house in Pompeii, like other Roman town houses, was based around the atrium—a pillared hall with a central roof opening.*

Seventeen years later there were more earth tremors in the region, but the people of Pompeii ignored them and went on with their daily lives. They had no idea what was about to happen.

On August 24, 79 A.D., Mount Vesuvius erupted. A violent explosion of hot volcanic ash and dust, small pumice stones, and larger chunks of lava suddenly rained down on Pompeii. In the streets the air was filled with poisonous fumes as the sky turned dark. Some people tried to take shelter, others ran for their lives as the city was buried under about 16 ft (5m) of ash and lava. When this volcanic debris hardened, it sealed up much of the city. Survivors fled as further eruptions shook the region, and the nearby city of Herculaneum was also smothered by a flow of lava and mud.

PLASTER PEOPLE OF POMPEII

Giuseppe Fiorelli found many skeletons during his excavations in the lava at Pompeii. He realized that the victims' bodies had made hollows in the ash and pumice, which had then hardened before the bodies and clothing decayed over the years. These hollows, or spaces, were like the molds that sculptors use, and Fiorelli devised an ingenious method of filling them to make copies of the bodies.

He poured liquid plaster into a hollow, and when the plaster set and hardened, he chipped away the surrounding lava to reveal the plaster cast. This cast was a detailed copy of the individual, sometimes even including an expression of fear or agony on the victim's face. Casts were made of people and animals, including a dog that had been chained up and was unable to run away. Many of the victims were trying to cover their faces with their hands or clothing as they suffocated. Casts were also made of doors, shutters, and even tree roots.

Altogether, about 2,000 bodies have been found at Pompeii out of a total population of about 20,000. Many citizens must have managed to escape to the surrounding countryside, but there may also be still more bodies to be discovered.

Pompeii was gone. It was buried and then totally forgotten, though in later centuries local farmers spoke of a "lost city" and found pieces of pottery and other ancient traces. In 1594 workmen building an aqueduct in the region uncovered ruined buildings. Then in 1709 a local farmer found large slabs of marble while digging a well. This started a hunt for buried treasure, and many valuable items must have been found and taken. Thirty years later an engineer named Rocco Alcubierre used strong tools and gunpowder to tunnel through the solid lava. He immediately discovered wall paintings and the steps of an amphitheater.

KEEPING RECORDS

For more than 100 years most of the people who visited the site were only interested in finding valuable pieces of treasure. Then in 1860 Giuseppe Fiorelli took control of the excavations. He began investigating the city block by block, keeping accurate records of all the finds at the site. He numbered every doorway, so that each house and shop could be identified. Whenever possible, he left things where they were found, so that it became easier to build up a picture of the whole community. Excavations have continued steadily since then, with occasional breaks.

We have learned a great deal about the events of August 79 A.D. from the writings of Pliny the Younger, who was staying at the nearby town of Misenum.

▶ *The Forum Baths shown here were one of three public baths in Pompeii. Roman baths had several rooms, each at a different temperature. This is the caldarium, which was hot, but not as steamy as the laconicum.*

▶ *The map on the right shows the location of Pompeii, while the map below shows how lava from the eruption spread to cover both Pompeii and Herculaneum.*

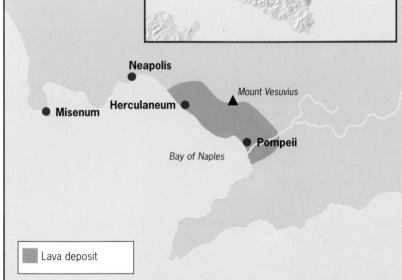

Lava deposit

Pliny the Younger describes in a letter how his uncle died:

“ My uncle went to rest in a house near the shore. Soon ash was piling up outside the door, making it difficult to get out. People could not decide whether to stay indoors or run away. My uncle tried to escape. Although it was daytime, it was darker than it is at night. When my uncle reached the sea, he found that it was too wild to set sail. The air was thick with flames as a great fire moved toward them. He stood leaning on two slaves, and then suddenly he fell down dead, choked by the fumes. ”

His uncle, Pliny the Elder, commanded a fleet of ships that had rushed to rescue survivors from the sea and get a closer view of the volcanic eruption. Pliny the Elder was himself overcome by fumes on the shore and died.

Today's visitors to the site can see what daily life was like in Pompeii, since about three-quarters of the city has been uncovered. Buildings have been restored, with reconstructed roofs, and scientists have identified the preserved seeds of many plants and regrown the gardens that Pompeians enjoyed.

Pompeii was completely buried under a thick layer of ash and pumice

At the time of the eruption there were three public baths in Pompeii where men and women could bathe and relax. Some wealthy citizens had their own luxurious bathroom at home. There were two theaters—a large open building for plays that held about 5,000 spectators, and a smaller, enclosed building for concerts and recitals. The amphitheater, where gladiators fought and killed each other as well as wild animals, has also been fully excavated.

In 79 A.D. the Harbor Gate of the walled city of Pompeii was only 1,650 ft (500m) from the Bay of Naples. The eruption flung ash and lava into the bay, and Pompeii is now a mile and a half (2km) inland. This shows the force of the disaster that buried a city and created a unique archaeological site.

SEE ALSO:

◆ ROME
◆ THEATER AND DRAMA

POTTERY

◀ *This present-day Egyptian potter is shaping a clay pot on a potter's wheel in the traditional manner that has not changed for centuries. The wheel is turned with a foot pedal, which is faster than turning it by hand.*

One of the earliest skills that people learned was how to make clay pots. When hunter-gathering people started to settle in one place, they found they needed vessels for cooking and serving food. The oldest pottery known was found at Shimomouchi in Japan—it is 12,000 years old. The pots were probably used to cook acorns; some still have soot on them from the ancient hearths. In China pottery of nearly the same age has been found at several sites, and it is thought that these pots were used for cooking seeds, including rice.

At Çatal Höyük in Anatolia pottery has been found that is about 8,000 years old, making it the earliest known Middle Eastern pottery. The potters of Çatal Höyük shaped clay into models of animals and humans for seals and pendants and into pottery vessels.

First, they mixed the clay with fine grit to strengthen it. Then they formed the mixture into coils, which were built up to form a pot on a round base. A paddle and anvil (round stone) were used to shape the vessel. After a few days, when the clay had completely dried out, the potter used a bone or stone to polish the surface of the pot before firing it in a kiln.

The earliest potters used very simple techniques for decorating their pots. One was impressing—fingers were pressed into the wet clay to make marks, or, as in some early Japanese pottery, a rope was used to make the impressions.

Another technique was incising—designs were scratched into the wet clay with a thumbnail or a pointed stick. This was the type of decoration used on Linear Pottery, which was produced by potters in Neolithic Europe in the sixth millenium B.C.

Later, slip (clay and water mix) and glazes were used to color pottery. The earliest form of decoration in Egypt, for example, was stylized animals and

EARTHENWARE AND STONEWARE

The first pots that people made were earthenware. People discovered that by molding clay into shapes and leaving them to dry in the sun, they could make vessels for holding dry goods. However, these pots could not be used for storing liquids since the clay vessel absorbed the liquid and eventually collapsed. Rather stronger pots could be made by baking the clay so that it hardened. At first the clay pots were just stacked in a hole in the ground, and wood was piled over them and set alight. Later potters invented the kiln. It was an oven in which the clay objects were stacked and then heated by burning wood underneath the kiln. Pots that had been fired were stronger than sun-dried ones, but they were still slightly porous (that is, they let liquids seep through slowly).

After the discovery of glass, glazes were used to make pots waterproof. The glaze was a coating made from powdered glass in water that was painted onto the earthenware. The pots were then fired a second time, and the heat fused the glass particles into a fine layer, making the pots waterproof and easy to clean. Glazes could also be used to color and decorate the pots.

Much later, around 1400 B.C., people discovered how to make stoneware. It is pottery that is fired at such a high temperature that it vitrifies—a chemical change takes place, and the pots become glasslike and completely waterproof. Because stoneware is nonporous,

▲ *This earthenware pot from China dates back to 5000–3000 B.C. The clay was coiled and the design painted on with a brush.*

it does not need to be glazed, except for decorative purposes. The first stoneware was made during the Shang dynasty in China and was being made in Korea by the time of the Silla dynasty (57 B.C.–918 A.D.). Stoneware was not produced in Europe until the 16th century A.D.

◀ *This powerful figure of a large, pregnant earth-goddess seated on a throne of leopards comes from Çatal Höyük in Anatolia. The clay was molded and shaped by hand in about 6000 B.C.*

scenes from daily life painted in white slip on a red clay background.

The potter's wheel was invented at the beginning of the fourth millennium B.C. in Mesopotamia. It was being used by potters in Egypt around 2500 B.C. There is no evidence that potters in the Americas ever used the wheel; most of their pots were molded (shaped in or over an object like a stone or a basket). The first pottery wheels were probably turned by hand, but eventually wheels with faster foot pedals were developed.

In the area around the Aegean Sea the potter's art seemed to flourish, producing outstanding examples of pottery from early Neolithic times to the wonderful sixth to fourth century B.C. Attic pots of Greece. Neolithic pottery from the island of Crete, for example, is remarkable for its finely polished surface and incised patterns.

During the Bronze Age civilization of the Minoans (2500–1700 B.C.) the potters who worked in the palace of Knossos on Crete produced some of the finest pottery ever made. It is called Kamares ware after the cave in which it was first found.

The clay used to make this ware had to be very carefully chosen, then it was moistened and kneaded over many months before it was shaped. At some

The ancient Greeks produced outstandingly beautiful pottery

point Minoan potters discovered the wheel and were able to make their cups so thin that an ancient Greek source described them as being "light as the wind, as thin as skin."

One of the loveliest features of these delicate ceramics was the floral decoration painted onto the small, one-handled cups; the paint actually strengthened the eggshell-thin vessels. The red-and-yellow designs included plant motifs, fish, octopus, and frogs. The work-shops at the palace of Phaestos on Crete used a great variety of patterns, with a profusion of spirals, rosettes, and lattices. These exquisite vessels were in great demand, and exports have been found in palaces on the mainland of Greece and south as far as Egypt.

The Mycenaeans (1600–1100 B.C.) also produced fine pottery that was heavily influenced in style by the Minoans. Mycenaean vases were exported to Egypt, the eastern Mediterranean area, and as far west as Italy and Sicily. With the end

▼ *A Mycenaean drinking cup from the island of Rhodes. The Mycenaeans produced great quantities of elegant pottery decorated, like this goblet, with abstract designs.*

of the Dark Ages (about 1100–800 B.C.) and the rise of the Greek city-states simple geometric patterns were gradually replaced by decorative bands of animals and humans.

ATTIC WARE

From about 550 to 300 B.C. pottery made in Athens dominated the market. These pots, known as black-figure and red-figure ware, were beautifully proportioned and decorated. They had a red-orange surface produced by mixing red ocher with the clay. For the black-figure ware the figures were painted on the red clay with a shiny black pigment. For the red-figure vases the artist outlined the figures in black on the red background and then filled in the whole background with black paint, leaving the figures red.

The artists who painted the ware were highly skilled and produced vivid scenes of daily life and episodes from myths and legends. Attic potters did not use glaze or varnish, and the method they used to get such a high gloss on their pottery is still a total mystery today. Attic ware was highly valued and widely traded.

The Romans made a type of pottery known as Samian ware by pressing the clay into a mold with impressed designs. This produced red pottery with raised designs. Many potters put their own name into the mold, so we know exactly whose factory a pot came from. The early ones were molded in Italy, at Arezzo. But as the Roman Empire expanded, the pottery manufacturers followed and set up their molds and kilns in France, at Lezoux. Archaeologists

◀ *A black-figure Attic amphora from the sixth century B.C. The black figures were painted in glossy black pigment on the orange-red polished surface. Details were added by incising lines or with small touches of white. Athens was the principal center of pottery manufacture in Greece, and the spectacular Attic vases were widely traded.*

excavating Arikamedu in India were surprised to find Samian ware there, proving the extent of Roman trade.

The Roman legionaries also had a taste for fine wine. So potters made a special storage vessel called an amphora. When filled with wine, they were shipped all over the Roman Empire. Sometimes merchant ships were wrecked at sea, and archaeologists have found the amphorae stacked in the hold at the bottom of the ocean.

As societies became larger with more people living in one place, many additional uses apart from cooking were found for pottery.

CHINESE POTTERY

In China, Japan, and Southeast Asia, for example, beautiful vessels were made to carry food and drink for the dead. They were decorated with painted scenes and were made in a wide variety of shapes.

Some of the best examples come from a 3,000-year-old cemetery in Thailand called Ban Lum Khao. Dead children were placed in huge pots, together with miniature vessels and jewelry, then a lid was put in place. Men and women were buried with up to 50 red-painted vessels of unusual and attractive shape.

The Chinese invented a third type of pottery—porcelain—during the Tang Dynasty (618–907 A.D.). Porcelain is a thin, strong, translucent pottery made from kaolin (white china clay) and ground petuntse (a feldspar rock). Early examples were quite primitive, but by 851 A.D. an Islamic account of travels in the Far East tells of "vessels of clay as transparent as glass."

NORTH AMERICA

The most important early North American pottery was made in the southwest. All pots were made by coiling or modeling. In coiling, rolls of clay are added to a base and pinched together, whereas in modeling a pancake of clay is put over a form that serves as a mold. The first pottery was made by the Mogollon and Anasazi peoples, probably around 50 A.D. By 700 A.D. striking Anasazi pots

THE BEAKER FOLK

Around 2800 B.C. a people whom archaeologists call Beaker Folk spread across western and central Europe, possibly from Spain. They are known from their individual round burial mounds that contained weapons and distinctive bell-shaped pottery beakers with horizontal rows of incised decoration. Their burials show that they were a warlike people, who carried bows, daggers, and spears. It is thought that they gradually spread through Europe as they searched for copper and gold. The beakers seem to have been used as drinking vessels, probably for social rather than ceremonial occasions. In central Europe the Beaker Folk came into contact with people of the Battle-Ax culture, who also produced beaker-shaped pottery, but in a different style. The two peoples gradually mixed and eventually spread to eastern England.

▶ *This fine example of a bell-shaped beaker has been totally covered with an elaborate geometric design created by incised lines.*

POTTERY AND ARCHAEOLOGY

Fired pots do not decay or rot, which means that pieces of pottery are often found virtually unchanged after thousands of years. This means that pottery can tell us a great deal about the past.

If two very similar styles of pottery are found a long way apart, it is likely that there is some connection between them. This might be because people have moved, but it might also be because the pots were exchanged as trade items. The Attic black-figure and red-figure ware from Greece, for example, is so distinctive that it is easily recognizable. Examples have been found in widely spread locations, which has enabled archaeologists to build up a picture of trading links between civilizations at that time.

New ways of studying ancient pottery have been developed in recent years. One is a technique that measures the amount of light heated pottery gives out. This can tell us when the pot was made. Another technique involves cutting a very thin slice through the pot, so thin that you can easily see through it. It is examined with a special microscope to find out which particular types of mineral or rock are present. In many cases it is then possible to discover where the pot was actually made, which tells us more about trade routes.

◀ *This ceramic whistle in the shape of a figure would originally have been brightly colored. It is a typical example of the Mayan potter's skill with its expressive features, big earrings, and decorated robe.*

with geometric black-and-white designs had appeared, forming the basis for the Pueblo pot style. The Mississippians (700-1540 A.D.) modeled clay head pots, hunch-backed women, and animals, often as bowls for tobacco pipes.

Central American civilizations may have begun making pottery in about the second millenium B.C. Between about 600 B.C. and 1000 A.D. the Maya, in particular, made simple pottery with red and black designs painted on a cream or orange slip, as well as highly intricate ceramic items. Elaborate models were attached to pots—one has a lovely abstract design on the lid from the center of which emerges a fierce jaguar with open jaws and sharp teeth.

The Maya used molds to mass-produce figurines of gods and warrior priests. These figures give us a good idea of how people looked, what sort of clothes they wore, and the ornaments they preferred. The Maya also created wonderful works of ceramic art that combined molded sections with hand-modeled details painted in reds, ochers, blue, and white after firing.

SEE ALSO:

◆ ÇATAL HÖYÜK
◆ GREECE
◆ MAYA
◆ MESOPOTAMIA
◆ MINOANS
◆ MISSISSIPPIANS

RELIGION

◄ *A painting from an Indian palace showing some of the many gods of the Hindu faith. In the forefront is Vishnu. Originally a minor deity, Vishnu grew to be one of the most important of all the Hindu gods.*

We do not know when people started to have religious beliefs. However, archaeological evidence suggests that humans may have practiced religious rituals as early as 50,000 B.C. In these early times humans were faced with an extremely harsh environment. Life was a daily battle against natural elements that people could neither understand nor control. Religion gave people a way of explaining the world around them, and its rituals gave them a means of influencing their fate.

Most early religions revolved around people worshiping a wide range of gods, each of whom was associated with a particular activity or force of nature. People would pray to sun gods or rain gods in order to ensure a good harvest, while sacrifices would be made to gods of war before an important battle. The worship of many gods is known as polytheism, and the ancient Egyptians, Greeks, Romans, and Aztecs were among the many ancient peoples to practice it.

One of the many ancient religions to have featured a wide range of different gods was Hinduism. Unlike

▲ *Siddartha Gautama—the Buddha—with two of his disciples. Born into a royal family, Siddartha gave up his riches to wander the land seeking enlightenment.*

At the heart of the Hindu religion lie the *Vedas*, a set of religious texts that include poems, hymns, and stories. The *Vedas* were composed between about 1500 and 600 B.C. and originally were passed down from one generation to another by word of mouth. Later, they were written down, and they are now seen as the world's oldest religious texts. They not only contain colorful stories about the adventures of a multitude of gods and goddesses, but also discuss philosophical ideas such as the nature of good and evil and the purpose of human life.

The Vedas *are now seen as the world's oldest religious texts*

A central concept of Hinduism is the idea of dharma, defined simply as "duty." According to Hindu belief, each human being has a prescribed duty to fulfill. It can be anything from being a slave to ruling a country. By carrying out their duties selflessly, Hindus believe they can earn reward in the next life when they are reincarnated.

BUDDHISM

Another of the great religions of the ancient world was Buddhism. Unlike Hinduism, Buddhism evolved out of the teachings of one man—an Indian prince named Siddartha Gautama, who was born in the sixth century B.C. According to legend, for the first 29 years of his life Siddartha lived a life of luxury, just like any other young prince of his time. Then one day, walking outside his palace, he came across an impoverished holy man who, despite his lack of worldly goods, radiated peace and happiness. Impressed by this sight, Siddartha left his riches behind

other religions of this kind, Hinduism has remained popular to the present day. Its exact origins are shrouded in mystery, but it is thought to have developed from a mixture of religions practiced by the people of northern India between 2000 and 1000 B.C.

HINDU GODS

Among the major gods worshiped by early Hindus were the war god Indra and Agni, god of fire. Gradually, however, the many Hindu gods began to be replaced by a trio of supreme gods—Vishnu, Shiva, and Brahma.

and began to wander the land as a beggar, hoping to find the same kind of inner peace as the holy man that he had seen.

ENLIGHTENED ONE

Eventually, after years of meditation Siddartha discovered what Buddhists call "enlightenment," an eternal state of happiness caused by freeing yourself from earthly desires. Siddartha became known as the Buddha, or "Enlightened One," and spent the rest of his life wandering across India with a band of disciples, spreading his message.

In the first few centuries after the death of Siddartha Buddhism grew slowly. But then in the third century B.C. the Mauryan emperor Ashoka converted to the religion, and it expanded rapidly. It quickly spread east, first to the island of Sri Lanka and then to China, Korea, Japan, and Southeast Asia. At this time Buddhism was unlike most religions practiced in the world in that it didn't involve the worship of any kind of supernatural deity. Instead, followers of Buddhism were expected to achieve the state of enlightenment through meditation, just as Siddartha himself had done. However, some later Buddhist sects began to worship the Buddha as if he were a god himself.

ZOROASTRIANISM

Like Buddhism, Zoroastrianism was based on the teachings of one man, in this case the prophet Zoroaster (or Zarathustra). Zoroaster lived in ancient Persia, probably some time between 800 and 500 B.C. Zoroaster was born into a society that, like most ancient civilizations, worshiped a variety of gods. However, Zoroaster established a new religion that worshiped just one

THE ROLE OF PRIESTS

Whatever form their religion took, most ancient civilizations had priests, religious leaders who conducted rituals and acted as intermediaries between their peoples and the gods. Most ancient peoples believed that their fate depended on pleasing the gods, usually through offering sacrifices. The priests who carried out these rituals were thus seen as very important, since the entire fate of their people depended on them.

Because of this it was usually very difficult to become a priest. In ancient Egypt, for example, apprentices had to study for many years before they were qualified. In other cultures only people from certain parts of society could study for the priesthood. In ancient India Hindu priests were taken exclusively from the Brahmin class.

Often, the duties of priests didn't stop with their religious roles. In many ancient societies priests were one of the few classes of people who could read and write. They thus often acted as teachers, scribes, and government officials as well. This gave them enormous power and influence in their societies as a whole.

▲ *An Egyptian chest ornament showing two priests performing a purifying ritual on the pharaoh Ahmose, using sacred water.*

The idea of single, supreme being opposing the forces of evil reappears in another of the world's great ancient religions—Judaism, which was founded in around 2000 B.C. According to the Jewish faith, the origins of the religion lie in a vision experienced by a Mesopotamian named Abraham, in which God (Yahweh) appeared to him and told him that his people had been specially chosen to spread his message on earth.

Central to Judaism were the Ten Commandments, given by Yahweh to the later prophet Moses. They gave strict instructions not only as to how people should worship the god himself, but also how they should treat their fellow human beings. Judaism thus contained a formal moral code that all Jews were expected to follow.

CONFUCIANISM

When we hear the word "religion," we automatically think of the worship of gods and goddesses. However, some religions also incorporate a set of moral instructions as to how people should conduct their everyday lives. In fact, one hugely influential ancient "religion" consisted entirely of a moral code. It was Confucianism, a system of beliefs that has now been followed for over 2,500 years.

Confucius (or Kongfuzi) was born in 551 B.C. in eastern China. He lived in a very turbulent period of his country's history, the so-called "warring-states" era. Confucius was a teacher and a philosopher (thinker), and he came up with a system of thought that he hoped would bring order and stability to his country. Confucianism stressed individual responsibilities such as loyalty and respect for one's parents. Confucius believed that if individuals behaved in a virtuous way, then society as a whole would be ordered and peaceful. Confucius also believed that

▲ A 19th-century illustration showing the prophet Zoroaster preaching to his followers.

supreme god—Ahura Mazda. Because of this, Zoroastrianism is often seen as a forerunner of later world religions like Islam and Christianity. Ahura Mazda represented a force of good and was engaged in a constant struggle with an evil counterpart called Ahriman. Zoroastrianism remained an important religion in Persia until the seventh century A.D.

rulers and governments had a responsibility to their citizens to rule in a fair and just manner.

TAOISM

Another ancient Chinese religion grew up at roughly the same time as Confucianism. It was Taoism. The

▼ *A Chinese painting of Laozi, the founder of Taoism. Laozi's teachings were often in the form of riddles.*

major figure behind Taoism was a philosopher known as Laozi (Lao Tzu), who was a contemporary of Confucius. Very little is known about the life of Laozi, and his teachings mostly came in the form of confusing riddles. Basically, however, Taoism told people to live as close to nature as possible and to accept and ignore the everyday problems caused by human society. As Taoism grew, it began to mix with traditional folk religions, in which local gods and goddesses were worshiped, becoming even more popular in the process. It has remained influential to the present day.

Taoism told people to live as close to nature as possible

In Japan a religion very similar to Taoism grew up called Shinto. Shinto was essentially a form of nature worship and was often practiced alongside Buddhism or Confucianism. Followers of Shinto believe in *kami*, a sacred power that is present in everything in the world.

Two other great world religions— Christianity and Islam—were to appear in the early centuries A.D., but they belong more to the modern than to the ancient world.

SEE ALSO:

◆ **CHINA**
◆ **GODS AND GODDESSES**
◆ **INDIA**
◆ **MAGIC AND DIVINATION**
◆ **RITUAL AND SACRIFICE**
◆ **ROME**
◆ **SHAMANS**

RITUAL AND SACRIFICE

A ritual is a ceremonial act that is repeatedly carried out according to strict, preset rules. Almost all ancient civilizations performed rituals, and it seems that they may have done so since the dawn of recorded history and before. By performing rituals, ancient peoples felt that they could help control the environment around them, and certain types of ritual were common among many peoples. For instance, rites of passage were performed at key points in a person's life, such as birth, the arrival of adulthood, and death. Festive rituals celebrated the coming of certain seasons. Sacrifices, meanwhile, were made to ensure the bounty and goodwill of the gods.

▲ *This mosaic from the second century A.D. shows a group of Romans performing a ritual intended to gain the favor of the gods of the Nile River in Egypt.*

THE POWER OF PRAYER

In most modern religions rituals are accompanied by prayers. Because of the absence of written records before around 3000 B.C. we do not know when people first started using spoken prayers to communicate with their gods and goddesses. However, written evidence shows that prayers were used in ancient Babylon and Egypt. In Babylon hymns to the all-powerful sun god Marduk have been found that date back to the second millennium B.C. It is thought that such prayers were recited on important days in the calendar such as the new year and the onset of spring.

Similar prayers were used by the ancient Egyptians, and many of them survive to the present day. These prayers took many different forms. Some simply praised the god concerned, while others asked for help in a particular area—people might ask the god to protect their family from illness or to help them in a war. Other prayers were recited at funerals and were believed to help the dead on their journey to the afterlife.

▼ The Minoans believed in life after death, so they buried people with food and personal possessions for the afterlife. This painting on a tomb in Crete dates from about 1400 B.C. and shows a procession of people bringing ritual offerings for the dead person.

The earliest rituals that we have any evidence of are burial rites. Graves have been found in southwest France that date back to around 50,000 B.C. They contain not only bodies but also tools and a number of other precious items. The elaborate ways in which these Stone Age people disposed of the bodies of their dead can be seen as a type of ritual behavior.

The people of the early Stone Age may also have had elaborate rituals to celebrate birth and marriage—but we have no evidence of them. However, we do know that such rituals were widespread in later ancient societies. The form that these rituals took depended on the society concerned. For example, the birth customs of the Aztecs reflected their warlike nature.

performed to secure their favor. The most valuable thing that could be given to a god was a human life, and so it is unsurprising that many ancient peoples practiced human sacrifice.

Human sacrifice existed throughout the ancient world. One ancient people who practiced it on a particularly large scale were the Aztecs. The Aztecs took captives from their enemies and then prepared them for sacrifice over days or even weeks. Then, one by one, the victims were taken to the top of a pyramid where Aztec holy men or priests pinned them to a sacred stone they called a *techactl*. The victims' chests were cut open with a stone ax and their hearts plucked out and held up to the sun. Then their bodies were thrown off the top of the pyramid.

The Aztecs sacrificed about 20,000 victims every year

These blood sacrifices were thought of by the Aztecs as an important ritual without which their whole civilization would be destroyed. According to their myths about the origins of the world and their special place in it, they were the favorite people of the sun god Huitzilopochtli. Huitzilopochtli had to fight a constant battle for survival against the moon and the stars so that he could rise every day and give life to the earth. As a result he needed to be fed with a constant supply of human hearts to keep up his strength.

Similar religious practices were very common throughout the world's ancient civilizations. In central America, for example, both the Incas and the Maya practiced human sacrifice, as did other Mesoamerican peoples such as the Olmecs and Toltecs.

When a woman gave birth, the midwife recited a prayer congratulating her for winning her "battle." The umbilical cord was cut and, if the child was male, was taken by an Aztec warrior who would bury it on a distant battlefield.

SACRIFICE

Probably the most important type of ritual performed by the people of the ancient world was the sacrifice. The word sacrifice comes from the Latin word "sacrificium" and means "to make sacred or holy." Sacrifices were offerings made to the gods and were

▲ *This 16th-century picture shows an Aztec priest holding up the dripping heart he has just cut from the living breast of a sacrificial victim.*

FEASTS AND FESTIVALS

Throughout the ancient world certain times of the year were set aside for feasts and festivals. Historians believe that these feasts even took place before the arrival of farming. Seasonal variations meant that food was more plentiful at some times of the year than others, and people celebrated these times by feasting. When farming began, these periods of plenty became more pronounced and the festivals more elaborate. In ancient civilizations such as Egypt and Mesopotamia festivals began to occur at several key points in the year, such as the beginning of spring or the harvest.

One of the earliest ancient festivals that we know about is the ancient Babylonian new year festival of Akitu, which was held from the second millennium B.C. onward. The festival occurred in the spring month of Nisan and lasted for 10 days. It began with three days of prayer, which ended with a telling of the story of creation. Some historians believe that it may have been performed as a play. Then a sheep was beheaded. Its body was thrown into a river and its head taken out to the wilderness. Then, three days later the king appeared. He was stripped of his royal robes and crown, and ritually humiliated by being slapped on the face. Having shown his humility to the god Marduk, he was then given back his royal clothes. Since the natural order had been renewed, the ceremony was concluded with a huge feast.

In Iron Age Europe certain Celtic tribes built huge wicker figures that concealed wooden cages. At festivals these cages were filled with sacrificial victims and then burned to the ground. Other human sacrifices were carried out by drowning and hanging. The method of death depended on which god the sacrifice was to.

CHINESE SACRIFICE

Human sacrifice was also widespread in ancient China, especially during the Shang period (1766–1100 B.C.). Like many ancient societies, the Chinese believed in an afterlife and thought that people had to be prepared for their journey to the land of the dead. Kings needed to be waited on by their servants, who were ritually killed so that they could accompany their masters to the underworld. Shang royal graves often contained the bodies of large numbers of beheaded sacrificial victims.

Many ancient societies, however, practiced animal rather than human sacrifice. In Greece, for example, domesticated animals such as chickens, goats, or cattle were killed. Usually, the

▼ *The base of a Celtic silver cauldron from the first century B.C. shows the ritual slaying of a bull. The warrior is about to stab the bull in the neck.*

flesh of the animal was cooked and eaten by the participants, while the bones and fat were burned as an offering to the gods. The sacrifice itself was only a small part of a far wider ceremony, which could involve music and dancing, processions, and prayers.

▶ *A red-figure Greek vase from the fifth century* B.C. *shows a couple performing a libation—pouring a small amount of wine into a dish over an altar in honor of a god. Most people in ancient Greece had an altar in their home and said prayers there every day.*

Another common sacrifice was the libation, a small amount of wine, milk, or oil that was poured onto the ground.

Different species of animal and bird were acceptable to different gods. If rituals were not followed correctly, the sacrifice might be rejected. Priests were responsible for making sure that everything was done properly.

SEE ALSO:

◆ AZTECS
◆ CANNIBALISM
◆ CHILDREN
◆ RELIGION
◆ TOMBS AND BURIAL RITES

ROME

The story of Rome begins about 1000 B.C., when people first started living on a hill overlooking the Tiber River in central Italy. The settlers belonged to a people called Latins, who inhabited a region around the Tiber called Latium. They were farmers and herders, and made their villages on hills so that they were easy to defend against neighboring tribes. The Palatine Hill, where the Latins first settled, was just one of seven hills that were later to provide the setting for the magnificent city of Rome, the center of one of the greatest empires that the world has ever known.

▲ *The remains of the main forum in Rome. Forums were open spaces used as market places and to hold political meetings.*

ROMULUS AND REMUS

Legend says that Rome was founded in 753 B.C. by someone called Romulus, who gave the city its name. All Roman children were told the story of Romulus and his twin brother Remus. According to one legend, they were the sons of Mars, the god of war, and a Vestal Virgin (a servant of the goddess Vesta), whom he raped. When the babies were born, their mother abandoned them on the banks of the Tiber River. Fortunately, the babies were found by a she-wolf, who suckled them. Then a shepherd found them and took them home to be looked after by his wife and himself. The boys grew up strong and decided to found a city on the Palatine Hill—on April 21, 753 B.C. However, the brothers argued over who was to rule the city, and Romulus killed Remus. This was how Romulus, according to the legend, became the first king of Rome.

The first kings of Rome came from the Latins and two other peoples, the Etruscans and the Sabines. The Etruscans were a highly civilized people who built roads, temples, and public buildings in the growing city. They had a great influence on the people of the city, and their ruler Lucius Tarquinius, or Tarquin the Proud, became king of Rome in 534 B.C. Tarquin was an arrogant man, and the citizens of Rome came to hate him. In 509 B.C. they threw him out and decided that they would be better off without an all-powerful king. Rome became a democratic republic, which meant that it was run by people elected by the citizens.

ROMAN DEMOCRACY

The new Roman Republic was headed by two consuls, who were voted in each year, and they were helped by other officials and a state council called the senate. Not everyone could vote, however, and women and slaves were excluded. Ordinary working people, called plebeians, were not allowed to become consuls or hold a high office in the republic. These positions were held by patricians, noblemen who owned land and traced their origins back to early Rome. Since officials were not paid, only the rich could afford to become politicians. However, over the centuries the plebeians gained more rights, and soon after 300 B.C. they gained equality under Roman law. By that time there was also a third, middle class, the equites or knights, made up

▶ **A bronze statue of the Roman dictator Julius Caesar. Caesar was a successful general, and his military power and popularity enabled him to seize political control of Rome.**

ROMAN CLOTHES

▲ *A mosaic from the fifth century* A.D. *showing a wealthy Roman lady being dressed by her slaves. One of her servants holds up a mirror so that she can see her hair and makeup.*

Romans wore simple clothes made of wool or linen. Men, women, boys, and girls all wore tunics, which were gowns that hung to the knees or lower. Men who were full Roman citizens wore a *toga*, which was a large, loose piece of woolen cloth worn over a tunic and wrapped around the body. *Togas* were usually white, although black versions were worn at funerals. Boys became citizens and put on the *toga* when they reached the age of 14.

Women wore a long dress called a *stola* over their tunic, and it came in a variety of colors. A large shawl called a *palla* was draped over the dress for outdoor wear. Women also dyed their hair—blonde and red were favorite shades—or wore wigs. Their slaves also helped them put on makeup, using chalk for whitening the skin and ocher for red lips and cheeks. Both men and women wore comfortable leather sandals.

of rich businessmen who did not come from a noble family.

The Roman Republic built up a strong, well-trained army and expanded rapidly. By the end of the third century B.C. Rome had conquered the whole of Italy. Between 264 and 146 B.C. the Romans fought three long wars against Carthage, a powerful city on the north coast of Africa. In the second of the wars the brilliant Carthaginian general Hannibal led his army of 40,000 men and 37 elephants over the Alps into Italy, but he and Carthage were eventually defeated. Romans were proud of their military power and their growing republic, but the gap between rich and poor was growing. This led to

THE ROMAN ARMY

In order to rule their huge empire, the Romans needed a well-trained, well-equipped army. By the middle of the first century A.D. the army was made up of 28 legions, each containing about 5,500 men (legionaries). Each legion was commanded by an officer called a *legatus*, who was usually appointed by the emperor, and was divided into ten groups called cohorts. The cohorts were further split up into centuries, units of about 100 soldiers under the command of a centurion. Centurions were responsible for training and discipline, which was important because the army had to put up with harsh conditions both in camp and on the march.

The soldiers in the Roman army were Roman citizens, but other men from the empire could join auxiliary forces and be granted citizenship if they fought well. When a new legionary joined the army, he was issued a uniform and equipment (that he had to pay for). A Roman soldier wore a helmet of leather or metal, a woolen tunic covered by a chainmail vest, and sandals. He carried a shield made of wood or leather, two javelins, and a sword about 2 ft (60cm) long. In cold climates he might wear trousers and boots.

When Roman legions were on the move, they regularly had to make new camps. They were expert at doing this quickly and efficiently, and the next day would take the camp down and move on. A Roman soldier covered about 20 miles (30km) in a five-hour march before stopping to build another camp.

▲ *A relief from Trajan's column, a stone monument that celebrates the emperor's military conquests. It shows Roman legionaries fighting Dacian soldiers.*

conflicts among political leaders, and in the confusion rose one of the greatest Romans—Julius Caesar.

THE REIGN OF CAESAR

Born about 100 B.C. into a wealthy family of the patrician class, Julius Caesar began his career in the Roman army before becoming a consul. In 58 B.C. he took command of the Roman armies in Gaul (modern France) and soon conquered the whole of that territory. Three years later he raided Britain. Caesar's growing power and popularity worried many Roman politicians, especially a rival general named Pompey, who was particularly jealous of Caesar. In 49 B.C. Pompey

---

After defeating his rivals, Caesar became "dictator for life"

---

persuaded the senate to order Caesar to disband his army. Caesar refused, and civil war broke out.

During the many battles that followed, Caesar showed his brilliance as a general. After an easy victory near the Black Sea he sent a message to the senate saying, "Veni, vidi, vici" ("I came, I saw, I conquered"). The civil war ended four years later when Caesar defeated an army led by Pompey's sons in Spain. Caesar was now ruler of the Roman world, and he declared himself "dictator for life." At a public festival Mark Antony offered him a king's crown, but Caesar refused it, well aware of the unpopularity of kings among the Roman people.

In the two years that followed, Caesar made many reforms that were to have a major impact on Roman life. He drew up a new legal code, reformed the calendar, created a police

THE COLOSSEUM

▲ *The Colosseum, probably the most spectacular of all ancient Rome's buildings. The amphitheater could hold 50,000 spectators who watched gruesome gladiatorial contests.*

Roman emperors, patricians, and plebeians all loved spectacular, bloodthirsty events, and one of the most important buildings in a Roman town was the amphitheater. In 70 A.D. Emperor Vespasian ordered the building of the most famous Roman amphitheater of all, the Colosseum in Rome.

The huge oval Colosseum took 10 years to build and was completed in 80 A.D. by Vespasian's son, Titus. It could hold 50,000 people and was built for gladiator contests, animal displays, and even mock sea battles, for which the whole arena was flooded. The Colosseum had 75 rows of marble and wooden seats in four separate tiers. The emperor and his guests sat at the front. Behind and above him sat patricians, then plebeians, foreigners, and slaves. Women sat right at the top, where they were protected from the weather by a huge awning.

Underneath the wooden floor of the arena, which was covered with sand to absorb blood, was a network of passages. Here there were rooms for the gladiators and other performers, and dens for wild animals. The Romans enjoyed watching gladiators kill animals and considered this great sport. On the Colosseum's opening day 5,000 animals were slaughtered, including lions, tigers, leopards, and elephants. Criminals were also killed by being thrown into the arena and attacked by lions.

Most gladiators were slaves captured in war. They were trained to fight in schools paid for by patricians. There were many different kinds of gladiator. Some, such as the *samnite*, wore heavy armor, while others fought with just a sword and shield. The popular *retiarius*, meanwhile, carried a three-pronged spear and used a net to trap his opponent. According to the Roman poet Statius, women sometimes took part too.

A wounded gladiator raised his forefinger to ask the crowd for mercy. Spectators waved handkerchiefs or pressed their thumb against their forefinger if they wanted to spare him, or turned the thumb toward the chest if they wanted him killed. If a gladiator showed great bravery and won a number of contests, he was sometimes given a wooden sword, which meant that he was a free man.

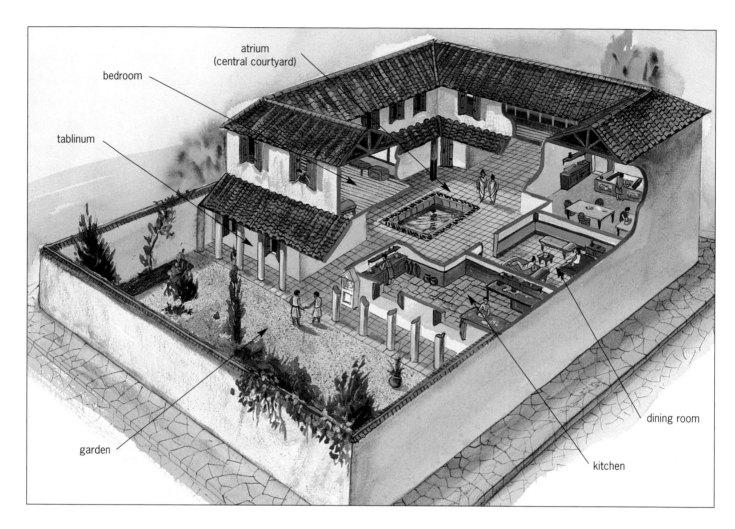

bedroom

tablinum

atrium
(central courtyard)

garden

dining room

kitchen

force, and took steps to reduce overcrowding in Rome. Despite these achievements, however, many patricians were unhappy at having a single ruler, and two noblemen began to plot against Caesar. On the Ides (the 15th) of March 44 B.C., the very day on which a fortune-teller had warned Caesar to be careful, the conspirators stabbed him to death outside the senate house.

THE FIRST EMPEROR

Seventeen years after the death of Julius Caesar his adopted son and heir Octavian became the first Roman

emperor. He took the name Augustus, meaning "revered" or "respected." The senate and consuls remained in office, but all real power rested with Augustus. He made sure that the boundaries of his empire were well defended and that the Roman

▲ *A cutaway drawing of a Roman town house, showing the rooms grouped round the atrium.*

▶ *A drawing showing how the Romans' central heating system worked. A fire burning in a grate in the basement circulated hot air under the floor and up cavity walls.*

CHRISTIANITY

For hundreds of years the religion of Christianity existed alongside traditional Roman beliefs. However, the followers of this religion were persecuted since its beginnings in the first century A.D. Because Christians usually lived in close-knit communities, they were often disliked by other Roman citizens and encountered much prejudice. Magistrates could order suspected Christians to perform pagan rites, and if they refused, they could be put to death.

Despite this treatment, Christianity flourished, and by the third century A.D. there were many large Christian communities throughout the Roman world. By now Christians could be found at every level of Roman society. In 312 A.D. the emperor Constantine dreamed that if he painted the Christian symbol of a cross on the shields of his soldiers, he would win a decisive battle. The dream came true. After this Constantine became more and more closely involved with the Christian church, surrounding himself with Christian advisors and putting the religion's symbol on the empire's coins. He was eventually baptized on his deathbed in 337 A.D., making him the first Christian emperor.

provinces around Europe were under control. Before he died, in 14 A.D., Augustus groomed his stepson Tiberius to take over as the second emperor. This move prepared the way for a succession of emperors who would rule the Roman Empire for a total of almost 500 years.

Augustus and Tiberius were both highly capable politicians and ruled the empire well. However, the third emperor, Caligula, quickly built up a reputation for cruelty and eccentric behavior. He is famous for making his favorite horse a consul and building a special palace for it. The senate found it difficult to control the bizarre behavior of their leader, and Caligula was assassinated in 41 A.D. His uncle, Claudius, replaced him.

CLAUDIUS AND NERO

Claudius was a scholarly man who wrote histories of the Etruscans and Carthaginians. His armies invaded Britain in 43 A.D., and he added other provinces to the empire. Claudius did much to improve the Roman civil service, the group of men who managed the nonmilitary activities

▼ *A mosaic from the third century A.D. showing two Romans buying wine from drink sellers. Street vendors like these were a common sight in Rome.*

of the government, such as collecting taxes and constructing public buildings. Claudius's adopted son Nero was only 16 when he became the next emperor, but he was more interested in acting, music, and chariot-racing than ruling the empire. Nero was another emperor famed for his cruel behavior. He was suspected of being responsible for starting a great fire that in 64 A.D. almost destroyed Rome. Nero blamed it on the Christians and tortured many of them to death. He eventually committed suicide.

In order to be able to move quickly throughout the empire, the Romans built first-class roads. They chopped down woods, cut into hillsides, built bridges, and drained marshes so that their roads could be as straight as possible. These roads replaced the winding tracks that they found in many of the provinces of their new empire. Roman roads were made by digging a ditch, filling it with rubble, and laying flat stone slabs on top. The roads were slightly arched in the middle, so that water drained off. Many modern roads throughout Europe still follow the direct routes taken by the Romans, which covered about 50,000 miles (80,000km).

As the Romans traveled throughout their empire, they began to adopt gods and goddesses worshiped in other regions. In Egypt, for example, they adopted the goddess Isis. In Persia there was Mithras, and in Britain the Celtic sun-goddess Sul. Since early times the Romans had believed that gods and goddesses were everywhere and controlled human actions. They made offerings and prayed to these gods, so that they would be friendly and helpful. Most important was the god of the sky, Jupiter. His wife, Juno, was thought to look after women. Other deities included Mars, god of war; Venus, goddess of beauty and fertility; Janus, guardian of the door;

▲ *The Roman aqueduct at Nerja in Spain. The Romans built many aqueducts— sometimes over considerable distances—to bring water to their cities.*

▶ *The extent of the Roman Empire at its height, after the death of the emperor Trajan in 116 A.D. Later Roman emperors found it increasingly difficult to defend the lands conquered by their predecessors.*

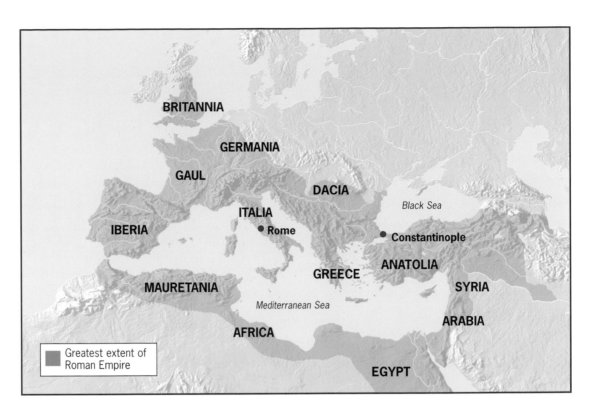

Greatest extent of Roman Empire

Ceres, goddess of the harvest; Mercury, messenger of the gods; and Vesta, goddess of fire. Many Roman emperors were also worshiped as gods, especially after their death.

Every Roman home had a shrine with small images of household gods. They were guardian spirits who looked after the family. Roman children were brought every morning to worship Vesta at the hearth, and this was an important part of family life.

DAILY LIFE

In Rome itself only rich patricians could afford their own separate house. Most people lived in an apartment block called an *insula* (meaning "island"). Some blocks were five or six stories high. The lower floors had large, comfortable rooms, but higher up they were smaller and more basic. On the ground floor there were usually shops or businesses opening onto the street. Richer houses were built around an inner courtyard, and the most important room in the house was the *tablinum*, the main living room.

Water supply was very good in the city of Rome and in all Roman towns. Aqueducts were built to bring water from nearby rivers or springs, and many patricians had water supplied directly to their homes. For everyone else there were public lavatories and baths, and larger towns had several.

HOUSEHOLD SLAVES

Better-off Romans led a comfortable life at home, which was only possible because they had slaves. The wife and mother of a family ran the domestic side of the household, and so she was in charge of the slaves. Household slaves were usually treated well, but they were not protected by the law, and their mistress could work them as hard as she wanted. A rich family could own dozens of slaves, and even poorer families usually had at least one. Slaves could be tortured if they behaved badly, and the Roman poet Juvenal wrote of slave girls being beaten for not doing their mistress's hair properly. Sometimes slaves were set free for good service. A freed man or woman did not have the same rights as other people, but their children became full Roman citizens.

At the height of the empire the city of Rome had about a million inhabitants, and in the rest of Italy there were a further five million people. Up to 70 million people were scattered throughout the Roman Empire, and the majority in the Roman world lived by farming. Some rich city-dwellers grew even richer by owning farms, where they built large country villas. In the fertile valleys near Rome itself farmers grew wheat, rye, and barley. On hillsides they planted olive groves and vineyards, for olive oil and wine, and grazed sheep and goats. The second largest city in the empire, Alexandria in Egypt, also shipped vast quantities of grain to Rome.

THE FALL OF ROME

The enormous size of the empire made it difficult to run from Rome, and eventually some of the provinces were invaded. In the third century A.D. a Germanic people known as the Goths invaded Roman territory in Greece, while the Persians overran Mesopotamia and Syria. In 330 Emperor Constantine moved his capital to Byzantium and named it Constantinople (it is now Istanbul, in

ROMAN BATHS

▲ *A luxurious, heated public bath built by the Romans in the city of Bath, England.*

Roman emperors built luxurious public baths decorated in marble and gold, which were popular not only for bathing but for exercising and simply meeting friends. The larger baths had separate pools for men and women, while others had special times set aside for each sex. There were cold pools, warm pools, hot steam rooms, and warm fountains for washing.

The Romans believed that it was good to sweat out dirt. They had no soap, so instead they made slaves rub oil into their perspiring skin and then scrape it clean with a curved instrument made of metal, bone, or wood.

The baths were available to everyone, and they usually cost one *quadrans* (a "quarter"), the smallest Roman coin. Sometimes even this cost was met by the emperor or a rich city sponsor. Large numbers of slaves kept the baths working properly. Heat was produced in a wood-burning furnace that blew hot air under the floors and up through the walls. This system was also used as central heating in richer people's houses.

Some Romans also brought their own slaves to the baths, to carry their towels, rub them down, and scrape their skin, while others hired these services at the baths. The public baths were used in a similar way to today's leisure centers and health clubs. As well as pools, there were usually sitting rooms, gardens, a gymnasium, an exercise field, and a library.

▶ *Roman villas, such as this one at Pompeii, were often built around a central open courtyard, called an atrium. Here the inner walls are decorated with elaborate wall paintings*

Turkey). Sixty-five years later the empire was split in two—the Western Empire, which was run from Rome, and the Eastern empire run from Constantinople.

The Western part was increasingly invaded by Vandals, Visigoths, and other Germanic tribes whom the Romans called barbarians. The Roman army suffered a series of devastating losses, and its generals were forced to make a succession of treaties with German chiefs that gave up vast amounts of land. The empire became so weak that in 410 the Visigoths sacked Rome itself. Then in 476 the Germanic chieftain Odoacer overthrew the last emperor of Rome, Romulus

Augustulus, and declared himself to be king of Italy.

Odoacer accepted the emperor in the East as his overlord. The Eastern, or Byzantine, Empire survived until 1453, when Constantinople was captured by the Turks. But the great empire built by the Romans came to an end almost 1,000 years earlier.

SEE ALSO:

◆ **ARCHITECTURE**
◆ **DAILY LIFE**
◆ **GOVERNMENT**
◆ **POMPEII**

SCIENCE

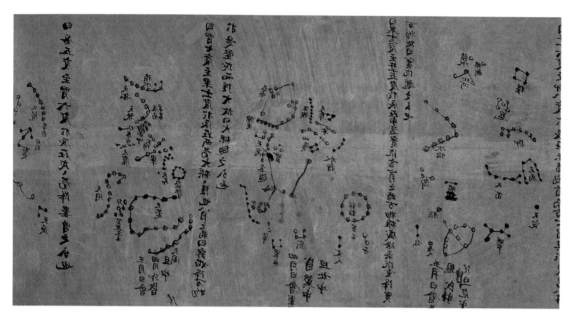

◄ *A Chinese map of the stars dating back to the fourth century* B.C. *The map shows constellations (groups of stars) linked by lines. The study of the heavens by the astronomers of the ancient world led to the study of mathematics— which in turn led to the study of engineering and science.*

Science is the study of the laws governing the physical world. It is known from cave paintings that humans made careful observations of the seasons from earliest times, while practical science began more than two million years ago, when our distant ancestors began making stone tools, showing they understood that if they hit a stone in a certain way, pieces would fall off to create a sharp cutting edge.

One of the first sciences to be studied systematically was astronomy. The movements of the sun, moon, stars, and planets were thought to reflect the actions of the gods and to predict important happenings on earth, so accurate observations were considered to be essential. This combination of astronomy and religion was the basis of early science in the civilizations of Mesopotamia, Egypt, China, and Mesoamerica. Careful observations of the heavens led to the study of

mathematics and to the development of sophisticated calendars like those of the Maya and the Chinese.

Mathematical knowledge enabled ancient civilizations to carry out ambitious engineering projects. Stonehenge, the great megalithic stone circle built in England in the third to second millenium B.C., was a major engineering triumph, involving the transportation of huge megalithic blocks of stone from great distances away, and then erecting them on site. The same skills were needed to build the pyramids of ancient Egypt.

WEAPONS AND WARFARE

Warfare inspired the constant invention of better weapons and defenses. The Chinese devised crossbows, scale armor (bronze plates mounted on leather), armor of quilted paper so thick that arrows could not pierce it, gunpowder, and firelances (a primitive type of gun)—all before 1000 A.D. The Assyrians excelled in devising siege engines, while the Greeks and Carthaginians perfected warships.

The needs of trade between far-flung peoples spurred improvements in shipbuilding, vehicles, and roads. Bridges—such as the suspension bridges constructed by the Incas in the Andes Mountains—were often masterpieces of engineering. The study of astronomy, mathematics, and the calendar often resulted in improved aids to navigation.

Surprisingly, water power was not used until the closing centuries B.C., when watermills began to appear in various parts of the world. The largest mills known at this time were built by the Romans at Barbegal in France. A set of 16 waterwheels supplied power to a huge mill that could grind 27 tons (24 metric tons) of grain per day.

Some of the basic elements of modern science were known by ancient civilizations but not understood. The magnetic properties of lodestone (magnetic iron oxide) were known to both Chinese and Western civilizations. The tomb of the Chinese Emperor Ch'in Shihuangdi (258–210 B.C.) was said to have been protected by magnetic doors that would capture any iron tools used against them. The Chinese also made bronze compasses with a central lodestone ladle whose handle pointed south. Greek and Roman priests, meanwhile, amazed the public by using lodestone to make statues of the gods float in midair.

ELECTRICITY

Natural electricity had also been observed. The Greeks, Romans, and Chinese knew that an attractive force (static electricity) could be created by stroking a piece of amber against fur. The Babylonians are said to have used electric fish as a means of anesthetizing patients. Some people believe that strange objects discovered in the cities of a Middle Eastern people called the Parthians may

▼ Stonehenge, a megalithic monument built by Neolithic people in the south of England, consisted of huge blocks of stone, some over 65 tons (60 metric tonnes) in weight. Its construction was a major feat that shows that its builders possessed great technical knowledge.

▶ *The Greeks used their scientific knowledge to build highly destructive weapons. This stonethrowing catapult from around 300 B.C. was capable of throwing boulders 180 lb. (82kg) in weight. Its power came from the huge amount of energy that could be stored in the twisted rope springs that held the arms of the bow.*

◀ *A traditional Inca-style rope suspension bridge over the Apurimac River in Peru. The engineering skills of the ancient Incas allowed them to bridge canyons as wide as 150 feet (45m).*

have been primitive electric batteries. These 2,000-year-old clay jars contained a copper cylinder sealed with asphalt into which an iron rod was inserted.

In about the sixth century B.C. some Greek philosophers (thinkers) developed a great curiosity about the way that the world operated and why. Aristarchus proposed that the earth moved around the sun (rather than the sun moving around the earth); Archimedes worked out that an object

names include Ctesibius, Philon, and Heron. Some of their inventions were of great practical value, such as the water pump devised by Ctesibius and Heron's diopter, a sophisticated surveying instrument.

However, although the scientists of Alexandria became familiar with many mechanical devices and scientific principles—levers, pulleys, screws, syphons, springs, cogs, and valves; the knowledge that hot air expands; the use of wind and steam energy—they used them mainly to make entertaining novelties and gadgets. Heron, for example, created a mechanism that opened temple doors as if by magic when a fire was lit by the priest on the altar outside. In fact the fire heated air in a concealed metal globe, which forced water out of the globe along a syphon into a bucket. As it filled up, its weight operated a pulley that opened the doors.

The Romans later made practical use of many of these mechanisms, such as levers and pulleys in cranes. Modern

always displaces its own volume of water; while Pythagoras figured out many basic rules of mathematics.

ATHENS AND ALEXANDRIA

Aristotle (384–322 B.C.) founded a school called the Lyceum in Athens that became the center of scientific inquiry of its day. Here the third century B.C. scholar Strato conducted many experiments into gases, some of which are still used to demonstrate that air occupies space. Later, the center of scientific investigation shifted to the city of Alexandria in Egypt. Its ruler, Ptolemy II (308–246 B.C.), a pupil of Strato, was a great promoter of the study of engineering and science.

In the encouraging environment of Alexandria many scholars conducted experiments in pure science—great

▶ *A decorative seismoscope, a device for detecting the source of earthquakes, made by the Chinese scientist Zhang Heng in 132 A.D.*

THE AMAZING ARCHIMEDES

Archimedes (about 287–212 B.C.) was one of the greatest of the Greek mathematicians and inventors. He studied at the Museum in Alexandria and then lived in Syracuse (on the coast of Sicily). A practical application of his work was the spiral-shaped device for raising water called Archimedes' Screw, which is still used today in Egypt to draw water from the Nile River.

One day when Archimedes got into a full bath of water, he saw that a quantity of water spilled out. He had discovered that an object displaces its own volume of water—and is supposed to have leaped out and run naked down the street shouting, "Eureka, eureka!" ("I've found it!"). Archimedes also discovered that almost any weight could be moved with relatively little effort by using a long lever and a fixed point, or fulcrum. He is reported to have launched the massive ship *Syracusa*—which had three masts and 20 banks of oars and carried 1,800 tons (1,633 metric tons) of cargo—single-handed, using a system of levers and pulleys.

Hiero, the ruler of Syracuse, employed Archimedes to prepare the city's defenses against possible attack. Archimedes replanned the city walls so that they incorporated devices for firing missiles, as well as new weapons with grabbing claws. When Syracuse was attacked by a huge Roman army, Archimedes' weapons kept them at bay for over two years. The Romans were pelted with huge stones and other missiles from giant catapults, followed by volleys of arrows. As they got nearer the city walls, the soldiers were crushed by boulders and large timbers. And worst of all, their ships were seized by giant claws that grabbed the bows, lifted the vessels, and then suddenly dropped them, capsizing and sinking them. Syracuse only fell in the end because drunken sentries allowed the Romans to gain entry. Archimedes was killed—to the dismay of the conquering general, who had hoped to benefit from his genius.

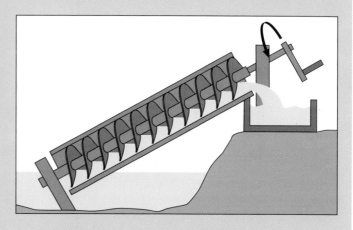

▲ *Archimedes' Screw, a device for raising water. When the handle was turned, water was forced upward by the spiral screw.*

scholars, however, have wondered why science did not develop further than it did at this time. One reason might have been that there were so many slaves that labor-saving devices were not considered important.

Scholars in India and China were also active in discovering how the world worked. The Chinese invented paper in the first century A.D. Around the same time, the Chinese scientist Zhang Heng devised a fascinating instrument to record the source of earthquakes. It consisted of a large barrel-shaped vessel decorated with eight dragon heads, each holding a bronze ball in its mouth. Beneath each was a model toad with its mouth open. When an earth tremor occurred, an internal pendulum would swing in the appropriate direction, making the dragon on that side open its mouth and drop its ball into that of the toad below.

SEE ALSO:

◆ **CALENDARS AND CLOCKS**
◆ **INCAS**
◆ **IRRIGATION**
◆ **ROME**
◆ **MOHENJODARO**
◆ **WARFARE AND WEAPONS**

SHAMANS

▲ *This Stone Age rock painting from Tanzania shows figures taking part in what may be a shamanistic dance. When the dance reaches its height, the dancers leap over imaginary animals that have been created in their minds by the power of their dance.*

In ancient civilizations a shaman was someone who was thought to have special powers and to be able to communicate with the supernatural world of the spirits. The term shaman comes from a Mongolian word meaning "he who knows." Shamans played an important part in the spiritual lives of the ancient peoples of central and northern Asia, the Arctic, North America, and some areas of Africa. In these parts of the world people believed that shamans could drive out evil spirits, heal the sick, and help carry the souls of the dead to the next, spiritual world.

A belief in the power of shamans was common among many peoples of the Arctic region. In northern Siberia many of the the nomadic peoples had shamans. It was generally believed that the magical abilities of the shamans were passed from one generation to another. A person did not choose to become a shaman but was chosen by the spirits before they were born. Physical deformities marked out future shamans from birth, and they could not hide from their destiny.

Shamanism was also common among the Inuit of northern Canada, Alaska, and Greenland, and each community had a shaman called an *angekok*. The Inuit believed that the spirits of people and animals lived in another world

DRUGS AND SHAMANISM

In some parts of the world, shamans used hallucinogenic drugs to help them go into a trance. Hallucinogenic drugs distort the senses and can induce visions and an emotional frenzy or make people enter a dreamlike state. The shamans in Mexico and the southwest of North America, for instance, considered the peyote cactus sacred and used parts of it in many rituals. The cactus contains a hallucinogenic drug called mescaline. So the shamans used peyote seeds to help them achieve the trance that allowed them to communicate with the spirits.

Similar hallucinogens were used by the shamans of other cultures. For example, to help them go into a trance, the shamans of Siberia would eat pieces of the large red-and-white hallucinogenic mushrooms that grew in the area. These

▲ *This painted textile is from the Chimu civilization of Peru (700–1476 A.D.) The humanized cacti plants in the lower corners produce a hallucinogenic sap used for "vision quests."*

mushrooms are highly poisonous and can easily kill a human being if eaten in the wrong doses. However, through years of experience the shamans knew exactly how much of the mushroom to eat and were thus able to induce visions without making themselves ill. Today, the use of such drugs is illegal in most countries.

after they died. Features of the natural world, such as the sun, moon, and wind, were also believed to have spirits. The spirit goddess of life, health, and food was called Sedna, and she lived at the bottom of the sea. The Inuit believed that Sedna sent out all the animals that they hunted, so she was very important to them. Only an *angekok* could speak to Sedna, and he might do so if the hunting season was going badly.

Like many shamans, the *angekok* went into a trancelike state before he tried to communicate with the spirit world. The Inuit shaman usually entered this trance by singing a rhythmic, magic song. Then he could visit Sedna, or even the great force called Sila, which the Inuit believed controlled every person and thing in the world. The shaman told the rest of the group what the spirits had said. If they promised a good hunting season, the community would reward their *angekok* with gifts. Sometimes, however, if he gave bad news or his forecast turned out to be wrong, the group might banish him from the community.

MEDICINE MEN

Many ancient communities had similar figures who were also believed to have special powers that enabled them to contact the spirit world. Among them were the medicine men of the Native Americans and Australian Aborigines.

The early inhabitants of North America had a great belief in the power of spirits to influence their everyday lives, and their shamans were believed to have close contact with the world of the spirits. As their name suggests, these medicine men spent much of their time healing the sick. They did this by holding special healing

---

Shamans who could talk with the spirits were very important

---

ceremonies, in which the shaman danced around the patient while in a trancelike state. The shaman might also blow tobacco smoke over the sick person because the tobacco plant was thought to have magical powers.

The Aborigines of Australia believed that everything that they came across, from people, animals, and plants to inanimate objects such as rocks, was connected to the spirit world. So people who could communicate with the spirits were very important.

An Aborigine had to go through very lengthy and complex initiation rituals in order to become a medicine man. In most of these rituals the candidate had to appear to die as an

▲ *This is a 19th-century illustration of a shaman from the Blackfoot tribe of North America.*

ordinary human being in order to make a journey into the other world and there, in a trance, learn the secret techniques of talking to the spirits. The new medicine man then returned to the real world to be reborn with superhuman abilities.

▲ *A medicine man of the Walpiri tribe, who live in the Northern Territory of Australia. The Aborigine people believed that the living could contact the spirit world through dreams or other states of altered consciousness.*

The Hmong people, who lived in the area that is now central China before the beginning of the Shang dynasty (1766–1100 B.C), worshiped spirits, demons, and ancestral ghosts, and their shamans had the main task of protecting them from evil spirits. The Hmong shaman was extremely important to the life of a village, since the people believed they were very vulnerable to the whims of these spirits. The ancient Koreans also had a strong tradition of shamanism. Their shamans were usually female.

AFRICA

In many parts of ancient Africa it was believed that specially chosen people could foretell the future. They did this by going into a trance and asking for help from the spirit world, or by examining the entrails of sacrificed animals. As in many early civilizations, people believed that illness and misfortune were caused by evil spirits. Medicine men and witch doctors, or tribal magicians, tried to heal the sick by magic and sorcery. Ritual dances, at which special masks and costumes were worn, were performed to help the healing process.

SEE ALSO:

◆ ABORIGINES OF AUSTRALIA
◆ MAGIC AND DIVINATION
◆ RELIGION
◆ RITUAL AND SACRIFICE

SHIPS

The first boats that we know about were those used by the early peoples who sailed from mainland Southeast Asia to reach New Guinea and Australia about 50,000 years ago. This means that the boat must be one of humankind's earliest inventions. Some of the distances these people traveled between islands were as much as 50 miles (80km), so the boats must have been fairly sturdy. However, none of these very early boats has survived. The earliest surviving boat is a hollowed out log dating from around 7400 B.C. that was found in Holland.

The first boats were probably made from hollowed out logs, but by about 5000 B.C. other types of craft were being used. They included canoes made of reed bundles lashed together and kayaks or coracles made of animal skins stretched over a timber frame.

Boatbuilding in ancient Egypt began with very simple rafts made of papyrus (a kind of reed), which was woven into a square and waterproofed with pitch. They developed into crescent-shaped boats with flat bottoms that were held together by a rope cable running from the bow (front) to the stern (back).

The Nile River, which runs from the heart of Africa into the Mediterranean Sea, was of great importance to the Egyptians. Because the winds normally

▲ *This fragment of a Minoan fresco (wall painting) from the 13th century B.C. shows a fleet of ships entering harbor. The Minoan war galley (left) was fast and elegant, with a high curving stem and stern, a ram, and a single row of oars.*

▲ Reed boats like this, similar to those made by the ancient Egyptians, are still used on Lake Titicaca in Bolivia.

blow inland against the flow of the river, the Egyptians could travel upstream on rafts with the help of a simple sail and then easily return with the strong current. In this way goods could be transported more speedily and easily than hauling them overland.

By 3000 B.C. Egypt was importing cedar trees from Lebanon, cutting

them into planks, and putting them together with grass ropes to make the first planked boats. Archaeologists have uncovered a ceremonial river boat that was buried near the pyramid of Cheops (around 2600 B.C.). The earliest plank boat known, it was well preserved but in 1,200 pieces. When reconstructed, it became a magnificent vessel 142 ft (43m) long and 19 ft (6m) wide. It was steered with enormous oars located near the stern.

From about 2300 B.C. Egyptian texts mention large barges that could carry heavy loads, such as obelisks (pointed blocks of stone) weighing up to 350 tons (386 metric tonnes). It is thought that some barges were over 200 ft (61m) long and 70 ft (21m) wide, and needed over 30 oar-powered boats to pull them.

MINOAN SHIPS

By about 2000 B.C. the Minoans on Crete had developed ships that had log keels, ribs, and planking joined at the stem and stern. They also began to

▶ In this Egyptian model of a sailboat (dating from around 1991– 1786 B.C.) the owner relaxes beneath the canopy, while the pilot stands at the bow. The earliest evidence of a boat with a sail of woven cloth dates from about 3200 B.C. The sail shown here is a modern reconstruction.

THE DRAGON SHIPS

The Vikings of Scandinavia were another great seafaring civilization. From the eighth to the 11th century A.D. they embarked on a series of raids and colonizing voyages that took them as far as the coast of North America. They built very long, narrow boats with a T-shaped keel, overlapping planks, a mast that could be raised and lowered, and a large rectangular sail. A steering oar—attached to the starboard (right) side on a block, fastened with a leather strap, and maneuvered with a horizontal bar—controlled the direction of the vessel. Oars were slid through closeable holes in the side of the hull.

Each boat could carry between 50 and 100 warriors on raiding parties. Their shallow draft (depth) and stream-lined shape meant that they could easily be rowed up rivers once they had made a sea crossing. To make their boats as frightening as possible, the Vikings put fearsome figureheads on the bow as well as gruesome faces on the stern, so that many called their boats the "dragon ships." Quite a few of these ancient galleys have been found by archaeologists because the Vikings buried their kings and leaders with their ships. One of these longships was over 300 ft (91m) from bow to stern and had more than 60 oarsmen. It was beautifully built, very narrow, and must have moved at tremendous speed. Such longships enabled the Vikings to launch attacks on large areas of Europe, including Scotland, Ireland, Britain, France, Portugal, and Spain, plus Russia and North Africa.

▲ *The Oseberg ship was part of a Viking burial around 800 A.D. Almost all the wood is original except for the upper part of the prow. It had 30 oars and was 72 ft (22m) long.*

▲ *An artist's impression of a Phoenician warship, which was low in the bow and had a heavy ram at or below the waterline. It was called a trireme because it had three banks of oars.*

▶ *The oarsmen in a trireme were positioned in rows, one above the other, with one man for each oar.*

build two types of ship. Warships needed to be speedy, to carry lots of men, and be capable of maneuvering quickly in different directions. The result was a long, narrow boat with a large number of oarsmen. Trading boats needed to be able to carry as much cargo as possible and also to be more seaworthy, so their hulls became rounded with high sides.

The Phoenicians came from a coastal strip now divided among Syria, Israel, and Lebanon, and their livelihood was based on trade. Some of it was by land, but most of it was by sea. They were the chief sailors of the Mediterranean between 1100 and 850 B.C. because of their seamanship and shipbuilding skills. The mountains of Phoenicia grew the cedars of Lebanon, which were prized for their hard, long-lasting timber.

The Phoenicians modeled their vessels on those of the Egyptians and Minoans, but also incorporated many improvements. Like the Minoans, they built a fighting galley with a long, pointed hull that was propelled by two or three banks of oars, as well as a wider, solid, ocean-going ship that enabled them to undertake ambitious sea voyages for trade and colonization. The Phoenicians sailed as far across the Atlantic Ocean as the Azores and even went around the Cape of Good Hope into the Indian Ocean.

then covered with a deck, which made the junk very seaworthy. Their sails were far ahead of those in the West. They were made of narrow panels stiffened with wood or bamboo battens. The sails had a rope at each end that could be fastened to a fitting on the hull. This meant that the mast did not have to take the full force of the wind and also that sails could be maneuvered to help the junk sail more into the wind. Western sailing boats did not develop similar fore-and-aft sails for another 15 centuries.

CANOES

The Native Americans were probably the first people to make birch-bark canoes. To do this they made a wooden canoe frame and then fastened large pieces of bark onto it to produce a long, narrow boat that could carry heavy loads and yet still be easily propelled with a paddle.

The Polynesians carried out some of the most amazing long distance voyages of any ancient civilization, crossing thousands of miles of ocean in partially open boats laden with colonists, animals, and seeds. Their voyaging canoes consisted of two hulls lashed side by side and propelled by paddles or sails. The hulls were either hollowed out tree trunks or, for the larger canoes, planks laid edge to edge and lashed together with rope. The canoes for local trips were a single dugout hull with an attached balancing outrigger.

In China log boats have been found that date back to the fifth millennium B.C. Sail seems to have come into use around the second millennium B.C. By the Han dynasty (202 B.C.–220 A.D.) the Chinese were using nails to fasten their planking. They also seem to have been the first to invent the rudder (a fixed underwater device that steers a ship). Pottery ship models from the first to second century A.D. clearly show rudders—a thousand years before the first European depictions of one.

THE JUNK

The Chinese also developed a design called the junk, which looked like a flat-bottomed box with a high stern and a massive rudder. Later versions were divided into compartments by bulkheads (solid planked walls) and

SEE ALSO:

- ◆ EGYPT
- ◆ EXPLORATION
- ◆ NAVIGATION
- ◆ PHOENICIANS
- ◆ POLYNESIANS
- ◆ VIKINGS

SLAVES AND SLAVERY

Slavery was widespread in the ancient world, and many civilizations relied on slave labor to provide a good standard of living for their citizens. Slavery was regarded as a normal part of life in most civilizations until relatively recently—it was not until the late 18th century A.D. that a significant number of people in the world began to believe that slavery was wrong.

A slave was a person who was owned by someone else—an individual or the state. A slave could be bought and sold, and had no legal or personal rights— they might have no choice about who they had children with and no say over what happened to those children. Families could be broken up at the whim of their owners.

Wars produced the most slaves. It was quite accepted that when one army defeated another, the victors had total power over the vanquished. Originally, most or all of the members of a defeated people would have been killed and their goods taken as booty. Later, it became more common to treat the people of defeated cities or tribes as valuable property and take them back as slaves or sell them to slave traders. Merchants followed the Roman armies to buy captured goods, including slaves.

BORN TO SLAVERY

The next biggest source of slaves was children born to slave women. Slave babies were taken from their mothers and given to wet nurses—women whose job it was to breast-feed them. Childminders then cared for the slave children until they were old enough to do useful work. Often, slaves were bred like animals so that the owner could increase the number of slaves he had, especially in times of peace when there were fewer conquests and therefore a smaller supply of captives.

A slave owner could make money from selling slave children. There is a record, for example, of a Roman who calculated that he had made a 10 percent profit on a woman slave by selling her children for a price greater than the price he paid for her and the cost of raising the children.

In addition, some people were made slaves as a punishment for crimes, children were sold into slavery by their parents as payment for debts or so they would escape starvation, and people even sold themselves into slavery, mostly to escape starvation.

SHORT-TERM SLAVERY

In some civilizations, such as Greece and Rome, there was an arrangement called "debt bondage." If someone owed money and could not pay, they might become a slave as a way of paying the debt back. This did not necessarily mean they were slaves for life—they might serve six or seven years before regaining their freedom. And sometimes there were people who deliberately sold themselves as slaves, taking a cut of the price, which they hoped to hold onto until they got their freedom again later on.

▲ *This Assyrian stone carving from the palace of King Sennacherib dates from about 700 B.C. It shows Assyrian slaves working in a stone quarry under the watchful eye of a row of armed guards.*

Hunter-gatherer societies seldom had slaves because everyone had an equal status. However, as people settled in villages and then cities and formed social classes, slaves became an important source of wealth and status. People had few machines or gadgets to help with everyday tasks, so slaves were needed to do most of the domestic work. Even humble families wanted to own at least one slave, since having none was a sign of failure. Slaves could also be owned by the state.

No one knows when slavery began, but by the time of the first written records it was firmly established in ancient Mesopotamia. When King Hammurabi wrote his famous legal code (around 1760 B.C.), it included a number of regulations about slaves. Most Mesopotamian slaves were members of the local population who had sold themselves or their children into slavery to pay debts; the rest were war captives. State slaves were housed in special barracks and used to dig canals, construct roads, build temples and fortifications, and work crown land. Private slaves were less common but were mostly used in domestic service.

SLAVERY IN EGYPT

In Egypt slavery had less importance because the peasant farmers provided much of the labor required to grow crops and build public monuments like the pyramids. Slaves were mostly foreigners who had been sold into slavery or captured in war. Egyptian slaves were reasonably treated (although their corpses were thrown into the Nile

River for the crocodiles). In addition to food and lodging they received a yearly allowance of clothing, oils, and linen, and their working hours were reduced in very hot weather. The personal slave of a high-ranking Egyptian had more wealth than most peasant farmers. Although they could be bought and sold, slaves could also rent land and become a "freedman of the land of Pharaoh" relatively easily.

Slavery is known to have existed during the Shang dynasty (1766–1100 B.C.) in ancient China. The Shang believed that slaves did not have souls, so they could be killed without penalty. By the Han dynasty (202 B.C.–220 A.D.) five percent of the Chinese population were slaves. Because there were large numbers of poor people to do most of the work, slaves were mainly a luxury item for wealthy people and might even become part of the family.

SLAVERY IN ROME

▲ *This first-century* A.D. *fresco from the Roman town of Pompeii shows a group of women having their hair done by a slave.*

The Roman conquests of the third and second century B.C. produced a flood of captives. A family measured its wealth by the number of slaves it owned and could afford to keep. Some Roman leaders had thousands of personal slaves, and the rich often owned several hundred. These slaves lived with the family who owned them and did the household work—washing their clothes, growing their food, looking after their children, tending gardens, and so on.

The government also owned slaves who did building and maintenance or worked as civil servants. On the whole, slaves were well treated, with the exception of those who worked in the mines, although there were a number of revolts when slaves rose up and attacked their masters. The most famous of these was in 73 B.C. It was led by a slave called Spartacus, who formed an army of about 70,000 before the Roman army defeated him two years later. Some slaves were paid wages and bought their freedom; others were set free as a reward. Under the emperors (27 B.C. onward) freed slaves became a large section of the population—many went into business, and others became administrators.

Slavery was widespread in many other parts of Asia as well. Korea had a particularly large number of slaves —from the end of the Silla period in 918 A.D. to the mid-18th century between a third and a half of the population were slaves. There were also large numbers of slaves in India, most of whom came from the local population. This was because their owners wanted to know which caste (class) the slaves belonged to. Most sold themselves or their families into slavery to pay debts or avoid starvation.

GREEK SLAVE STATE

In most civilizations slaves were a relatively small part of the population and did not play a large economic role; ancient Greece was the first civilization where slaves formed a large part of the population, and where owning slaves made a great impact on society—the family, the economy, and the law.

The first slaves were Greek; but when Solon abolished citizen slavery in about 594 B.C., people turned to war captives and trade. By the fifth to the third century B.C. about a third of the population were slaves, and slaves were responsible for Athens's wealth and the leisure of its citizens. Many slaves lived as part of the family, some became

▲ *A 19th-century drawing of a group of African slaves being taken to the coast by their African captors. Having been captured on a raid or during a war, slaves were often made to walk long distances. This group has been chained together, and one is being beaten, possibly because he is not walking fast enough.*

craftsmen who were paid for their work, and others led a wretched life in the silver mines of Laurion.

The societies of Central and South America—the Maya, Incas, and Aztecs —took thousands of slaves, but most were sacrificed to the gods to avert their anger and ensure good harvests.

AFRICAN SLAVES

Slaves have been owned in Africa throughout recorded history. Because much of the land was poor, livestock and people were a source of wealth. Kingdoms increased slave ownership through wars and raids, while individuals mostly wanted women and children for labor and to produce children who would become part of the family. Slaves were also traded in exchange for other valuable commodities, but it was not until about 650 A.D. and the rise of Islam that the slave trade began to involve thousands of people.

SEE ALSO:

◆ **AZTECS**
◆ **GREECE**
◆ **ROME**
◆ **SOCIAL ORGANIZATION**

SOCIAL ORGANIZATION

◄ *This eighth-century stone carving shows slaves carrying dishes to a meal for the Assyrian king Sargon II. The Assyrian labor force was drawn from conquered peoples, who had been forced to leave their own countries.*

The hunter-gatherer people of Paleolithic times had no concept of class distinction. While some hunters may have been especially valued for their hunting skills, everybody in the tribe was treated equally and shared in the food available. Even when these hunter-gatherers started to settle in villages and began to farm about 10,000 years ago, families worked together within the community as equals to build houses and plant crops. Women seem to have played a key role and may even have had a higher status than men because of their ability to bear children.

However, when people began to live in cities, different roles started to emerge. Some became merchants and traders, some skilled craftspeople, while others remained farmers. Gradually, different classes developed, which meant that people were no longer equally valued.

SOCIAL DIFFERENCES

The societies of ancient civilizations were organized in very different ways. A civilization's style of government had a major effect on the way its society was organized. There was a great contrast, for example, between the society of ancient Egypt, with its supreme god-ruler, and that of the city-states in ancient Greece, where citizens were expected to participate in the running of their society. Religion, too, played a key role. The priests were often one of the highest classes in a society, especially when religion was closely linked with the position of the ruler.

MESOPOTAMIA

In Mesopotamia the legal code of King Hammurabi (1792–1750 B.C.) describes three social classes—free men (*awilum*), state dependents (*mushkenum*), and slaves (*wardum*). Penalties prescribed by the code varied according to social class. A distinction was made between foreign slaves who were captives and those who were native born. Although they had no official status, craftsmen and tradesmen were subject to legal regulations and taxes.

THE SYSTEM IN EGYPT

At the top of the Egyptian system was the pharaoh. Beneath him was the ruling class—the hereditary nobles and the high priests. Below them were the scribes, lower priests and court servants, and later, soldiers. Apart from slaves, the lowest order was the agricultural laborers and miners. If someone had talent, it was possible, although not common, to improve in status.

The differences in burial rites reflected social class. Some early pharaohs were buried in special tombs called pyramids with fabulous collections of gold, jewelry, and other precious objects. Court officials, even minor ones, would spend much of their life and wealth preparing an elaborate tomb where they would expect to be buried with their treasures. Yet the body of a poor person was usually just wrapped in a piece of linen and left in the desert, a cave, or a pit with only a staff and a pair of sandals.

Ancient China was not one country but a number of kingdoms, each ruled by a powerful family. The first dynasty (ruling family) to leave a historical

record was the Shang (1766–1100 B.C.). Under the Shang dynasty the people were ruled by a supreme priest-king. Hereditary aristocrats lived in great luxury, while the common people lived in simple wattle-and-daub (clay-and-twig) houses. Worship of ancestors and family ties were key aspects of society.

FEUDAL SOCIETY

When the Chou dynasty (1050–256 B.C.) conquered the Shang, a feudal society was established. This was a system based on land ownership. Below the ruler were five ranks of noblemen. Each rank rented land from the nobles immediately above them, and all land was farmed by commoners with the help of slaves. The commoners were bound to the land and could not leave it, making them virtually the property of their lords.

The noble families held enormous power. At the head of each family was a powerful landowner. Then came his family, concubines (mistresses), servants, and slaves. Tenant farmers

▼ *An Egyptian tomb painting shows the Royal Scribe, Userhet, hunting gazelle. It was possible for a man of humble birth to rise to a position of authority in ancient Egypt, provided he had talent. Becoming a scribe was a good way to improve one's status.*

worked the huge estate. To defend the estate there would be a private army, often housed in defensive castles. In fact, these powerful families were really societies within a wider society, for they controlled not only many farms and villages but mines and manufacturing as well. Merchants had very little social status or power, and craftsmen were on about the same social level as soldiers and peasant farmers.

GOVERNMENT OFFICIALS

When the Ch'in dynasty (221–207 B.C.) took power, and China was united under Ch'in Shihuangdi, he reduced the power of the ruling families and introduced a new class of officials. At first, many of them came from the great families, but by the time of the Han dynasty (202 B.C.–220 A.D.) tests ensured that officials were selected on ability. Although the aristocratic familes retained a great deal of power, the value given to ability and education meant that people no longer had to remain

▲ *In ancient China nobles and relatives of the Chinese emperor lived a life of great luxury, as this painting shows. Servants and slaves carried out the domestic and agricultural work, allowing their lords plenty of leisure time to enjoy social activities.*

in the class they were born into but could improve their social position.

In ancient India social position was influenced by family, occupation, and feudal-style relationships; but most of all it was determined by the caste system, which had been introduced to India by the invading Vedic peoples around 2000 B.C. Each person was born into a particular group called a *jati* and had to marry someone within that *jati*. It was impossible to escape from a *jati* except by becoming a holy man. The *brahmans* or priests were in the top (purest) caste, while the *shudra*—peasants—were in the bottom (least pure) caste. Those outside the caste system were considered outcasts, and so "untouchable."

The caste system determined social position in ancient India

Despite their feudal and caste systems, India, China, Korea, and Japan were different from most other societies in the value they placed on learning. Through education it was possible, even in India, to improve one's social status.

In contrast to the states ruled by a powerful king, the main social division in the Greek city-state of Athens was between free people and slaves. Free men were divided into citizens and *metics*. A citizen was born to Athenian parents and was expected to participate in government whether he was an aristocrat or a farmer. A *metic* was foreign-born; and although he had some legal rights, he could never participate in government.

In 510 B.C. ancient Rome became a republic. The citizens were known as the *populus*. They were divided into

AN IDEAL SOCIETY?

No ancient civilization could be considered "just" in modern terms, but some scholars thought that the Incas of ancient Peru had developed an ideal social organization. So impressed was Montaigne, an 18th-century French philosopher (thinker), with what he heard about Inca communal ownership of land, its widespread and fair system of government, and its welfare care for the peasants that he wrote, "neither Greece, nor Rome, nor Egypt could show any comparison with the achievements of the Inca."

Was this the reality, however? Inca society was highly structured, with the emperor at the top. Governing officials were drawn from the royal family and the nobles. Land and goods were divided into those products owned by the Inca emperor, those reserved for the gods, and lands and products that could be used by the common people. There was no money, so value was measured by goods and labor. Everyone knew their place in society, widows and orphans were cared for by the community, royal officials oversaw village life, the state stored food reserves to feed the population in times of famine, and the army enforced public order. There was no place for envy or social climbing. Was this the earliest known benevolent communist society, or was it an oppressive dictatorship? Scholars have argued over the matter for centuries, but regardless of the answer, everyone agrees that the social organization of the Inca Empire was one of the wonders of the ancient world.

two major groupings: the patricians, who were the land-owning, governing class, and the plebeians, who included craftsmen, soldiers, farmers, merchants, and laborers. Provincials (people who lived on Roman territory but outside Rome) did not have the full rights of Roman citizens and had to pay taxes.

During the early republic there were few slaves, but the numbers soon grew. In 27 B.C. Octavian took the title Augustus and became the first Roman

▲ *This 19th-century picture shows the reconstructed interior of a Roman house with a patrician family chatting and playing, while their slaves do the domestic chores.*

emperor. Imperial Rome had a very complex and sophisticated society with huge numbers of slaves. There were different laws for the upper classes, who were called *honestiores* ("more honorable" men), and ordinary people. While the poor could be punished by being flogged, burned alive, or being thrown to wild animals, the *honestiores* had to be executed with a sword.

In most ancient societies women took the social class of their fathers and husbands, but the rights they enjoyed varied in different civilizations and at different times. Mostly they were subordinate first to a father and then to a husband or to other male relatives, and did not play an active role in society.

SEE ALSO:

◆ CHINA
◆ GOVERNMENT
◆ INCAS
◆ INDIA
◆ SLAVES AND SLAVERY
◆ WOMEN

TIMELINE

	6500 BC	6000	5500	5000	4500	4000	350

EUROPE

NEOLITHIC EUROPE: MEGALITHIC MONUMENTS 6500—1500
STEPPES: SREDNY STOG 4400—350

OCEANIA

ABORIGINE CULTURE 40,000 B.C.—PRESEN

**INDIA AND
THE FAR EAST**

AMERICAS

**MIDDLE EAST
AND AFRICA**

JERICHO 10,000—6000 B.C.
ÇATAL HÖYÜK 6250—5400 B.C.

MESOPOTAMIA 5000—3000 B.C.

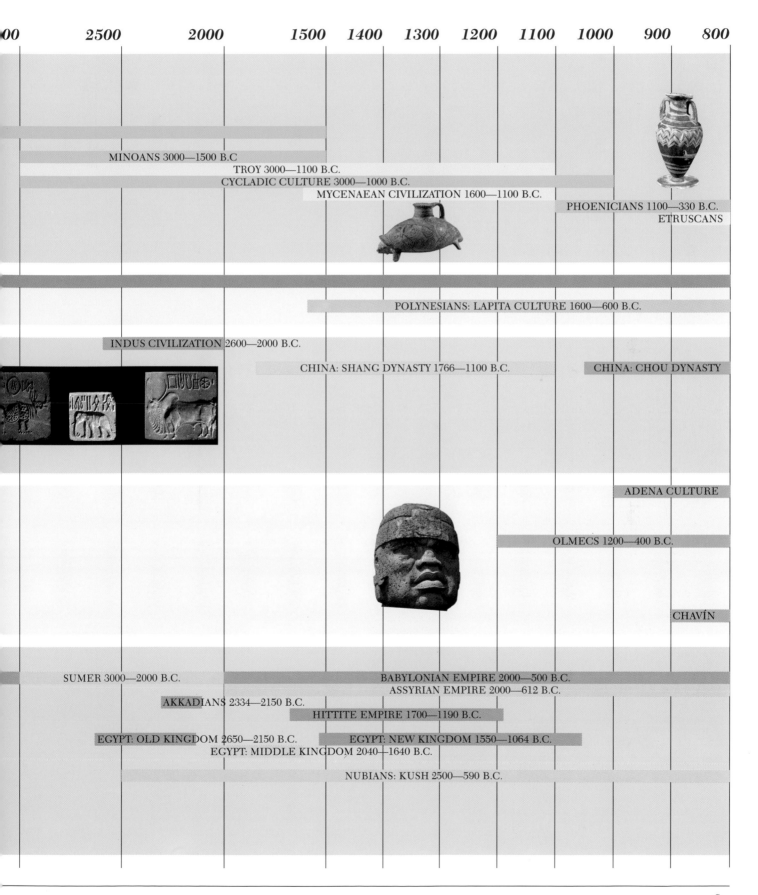

| 3000 | 2500 | 2000 | 1500 | 1400 | 1300 | 1200 | 1100 | 1000 | 900 | 800 |

MINOANS 3000—1500 B.C

TROY 3000—1100 B.C.

CYCLADIC CULTURE 3000—1000 B.C.

MYCENAEAN CIVILIZATION 1600—1100 B.C.

PHOENICIANS 1100—330 B.C.

ETRUSCANS

POLYNESIANS: LAPITA CULTURE 1600—600 B.C.

INDUS CIVILIZATION 2600—2000 B.C.

CHINA: SHANG DYNASTY 1766—1100 B.C.

CHINA: CHOU DYNASTY

ADENA CULTURE

OLMECS 1200—400 B.C.

CHAVÍN

SUMER 3000—2000 B.C.

BABYLONIAN EMPIRE 2000—500 B.C.

ASSYRIAN EMPIRE 2000—612 B.C.

AKKADIANS 2334—2150 B.C.

HITTITE EMPIRE 1700—1190 B.C.

EGYPT: OLD KINGDOM 2650—2150 B.C.

EGYPT: NEW KINGDOM 1550—1064 B.C.

EGYPT: MIDDLE KINGDOM 2040—1640 B.C.

NUBIANS: KUSH 2500—590 B.C.

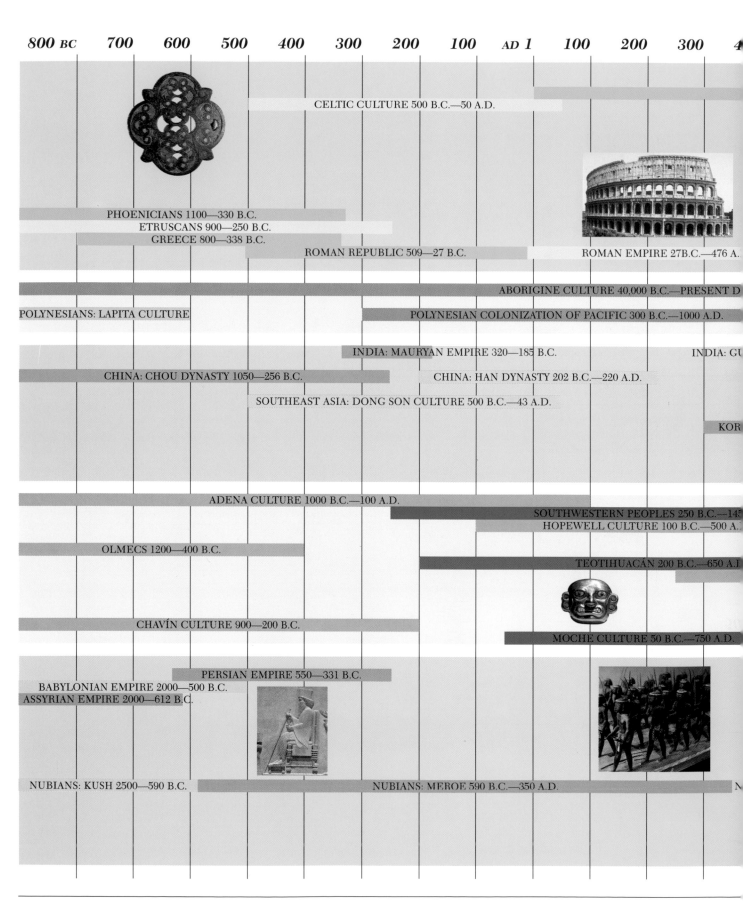

800 BC	700	600	500	400	300	200	100	AD 1	100	200	300	4

CELTIC CULTURE 500 B.C.—50 A.D.

PHOENICIANS 1100—330 B.C.
ETRUSCANS 900—250 B.C.
GREECE 800—338 B.C.
ROMAN REPUBLIC 509—27 B.C.   ROMAN EMPIRE 27B.C.—476 A.

ABORIGINE CULTURE 40,000 B.C.—PRESENT D
POLYNESIANS: LAPITA CULTURE   POLYNESIAN COLONIZATION OF PACIFIC 300 B.C.—1000 A.D.

INDIA: MAURYAN EMPIRE 320—185 B.C.   INDIA: GU
CHINA: CHOU DYNASTY 1050—256 B.C.   CHINA: HAN DYNASTY 202 B.C.—220 A.D.
SOUTHEAST ASIA: DONG SON CULTURE 500 B.C.—43 A.D.

KOR

ADENA CULTURE 1000 B.C.—100 A.D.
SOUTHWESTERN PEOPLES 250 B.C.—14⁵
HOPEWELL CULTURE 100 B.C.—500 A.
OLMECS 1200—400 B.C.
TEOTIHUACÁN 200 B.C.—650 A.I
CHAVÍN CULTURE 900—200 B.C.
MOCHE CULTURE 50 B.C.—750 A.D.

PERSIAN EMPIRE 550—331 B.C.
BABYLONIAN EMPIRE 2000—500 B.C.
ASSYRIAN EMPIRE 2000—612 B.C.

NUBIANS: KUSH 2500—590 B.C.   NUBIANS: MEROE 590 B.C.—350 A.D.   N

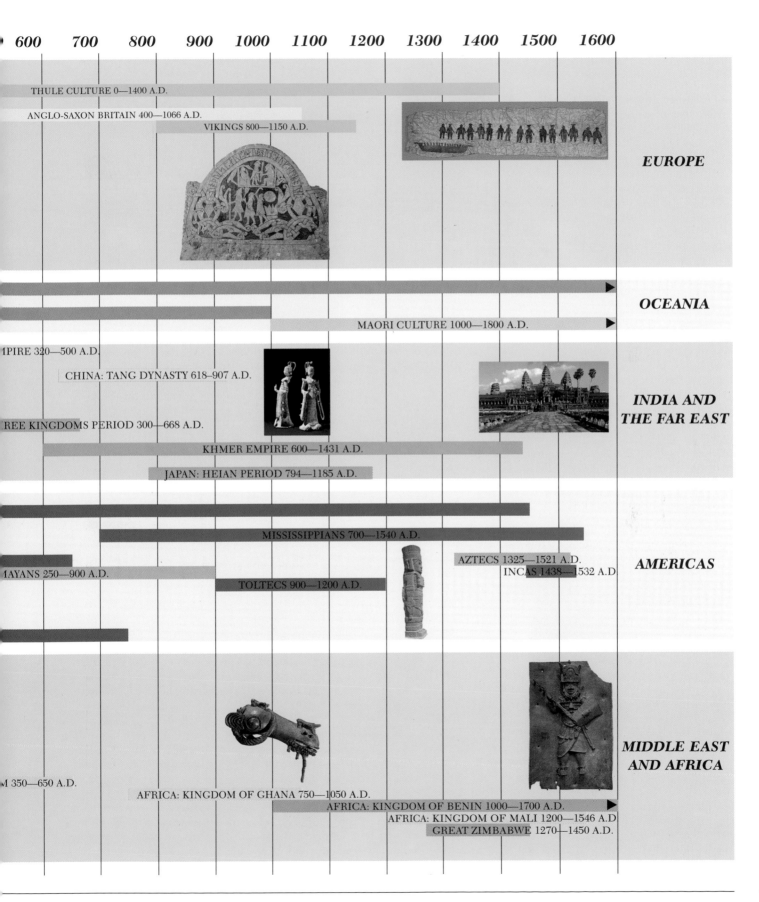

600   700   800   900   1000   1100   1200   1300   1400   1500   1600

THULE CULTURE 0—1400 A.D.

ANGLO-SAXON BRITAIN 400—1066 A.D.

VIKINGS 800—1150 A.D.

EUROPE

OCEANIA

MAORI CULTURE 1000—1800 A.D.

MPIRE 320—500 A.D.

CHINA: TANG DYNASTY 618—907 A.D.

INDIA AND THE FAR EAST

REE KINGDOMS PERIOD 300—668 A.D.

KHMER EMPIRE 600—1431 A.D.

JAPAN: HEIAN PERIOD 794—1185 A.D.

MISSISSIPPIANS 700—1540 A.D.

AZTECS 1325—1521 A.D.

INCAS 1438—1532 A.D.

AMERICAS

MAYANS 250—900 A.D.

TOLTECS 900—1200 A.D.

MIDDLE EAST AND AFRICA

M 350—650 A.D.

AFRICA: KINGDOM OF GHANA 750—1050 A.D.

AFRICA: KINGDOM OF BENIN 1000—1700 A.D.

AFRICA: KINGDOM OF MALI 1200—1546 A.D

GREAT ZIMBABWE 1270—1450 A.D.

GLOSSARY

A.D. Anno Domini ("the year of our Lord") was the year that Christ was born. All dates with these letters written after them are measured forward from his birth to the present day.

B.C. Before Christ. All dates with these letters written after them are measured backward from Christ's birth date.

Bronze Age The second period of mankind, after the Stone Age and before the Iron Age, when bronze tools and weapons were used. In Europe and Asia it lasted from around 2000 to 700 B.C.

Buddhism An Indian religion, following the teaching of the Buddha (enlightened one), based on the idea that humans can be freed from suffering by self-purification, known as enlightenment.

bureaucracy A governing body organized into a number of separate departments, each specializing in a different area.

ceramic An object made from clay or a similar material, usually by firing it in an oven.

city-state An independent city that rules territories that are subject to it.

consolidate To unite parts into a whole, or to strengthen one's power over a state.

cuneiform An ancient system of writing made up of wedge-shaped characters, especially that used in Mesopotamia.

domesticate Taking animals and plants out of the wild and changing them so that they become adaptable to human needs, to be used for food, materials, or transportation.

dynasty A series of rulers from the same family.

economy The resources and finances of a community or country, especially when they are managed by a central government.

freeman A person who is neither a slave nor a servant but is free.

fresco A wall painting made with water-based paints on fresh plaster.

funerary Items or places, such as tombs, associated with the burial of a dead person.

hierarchy The division of a social group into ranks or classes.

Hinduism A religion from northern India.

hunter-gatherers People in the Stone Age who existed by hunting wild animals and gathering berries, roots, nuts, and fruit.

Iron Age The third period of mankind, after the Bronze Age, when iron was the main metal used. In Europe it lasted from about 700 B.C. to 100 A.D.

irrigation A man-made system for bringing water to the land to help plants grow that was first developed in about 4500 B.C. in Mesopotamia.

megalith A very large stone, often used to build a structure such as a tomb.

Mesoamerican Describes the ancient civilizations that flourished in Central America in the region stretching from central Mexico to present-day Nicaragua.

metallurgy The method of either working with, or heating, metals in order to make new types and shapes.

millennium A period of 1,000 years.

molten To turn metal liquid by heating.

mud brick A brick made from mud that was shaped into a block and left to dry in the sun. Mud bricks were used to build houses in desert climates.

Neolithic Of the later Stone Age, when people started to farm and live in settlements.

nomads People who wander from place to place rather than living in a settled village.

omen An event that is believed to be a sign of future happiness or disaster.

pagan A term used by the ancient Romans and Greeks to describe people who believed in more than one god.

panning A process for finding gold in rivers; the silt from the river bed is washed through a sieve, leaving the gold behind.

papyrus A material made from an aquatic Egyptian plant. Before people knew how to make paper, civilizations such as the ancient Greeks, Romans, and Egyptians used papyrus to write on.

philosopher A person who constructs theories on the meaning of human life and other profound issues.

Pre-Hispanic A term used to describe the period before the Spanish conquest; usually in connection with Central and South American cultures.

relief A sculpture that is carved into the side of a wall so that it projects out of a flat background surface.

sack To plunder, or rob, and partly destroy a place.

Sanskrit An ancient language that has become the classical language of India and Hinduism.

scholar A learned person or someone who has undertaken advanced studies.

scribe Before the invention of printing, a person employed to copy documents by hand.

shaman A priest or priestess who uses magic to cure the sick, foretell the future, and reveal mysteries.

smelting The method used to separate a metal from its ore. It involves heating the ore to a very high temperature.

staple A basic food item or crop.

Stone Age The first period of mankind, before the invention of metal, when people used stone tools and weapons. In Europe it occurred between about 2.5 million and 2000 B.C.

symbol Something that stands for something else. For instance, a cross often symbolizes Christianity.

tribute A payment of gifts, money, or people, usually on a regular basis, by one state or ruler to another to show submission or loyalty.

vassal A person who has sworn an oath of loyalty to a king or noble. In exchange he may receive either protection or land.

FURTHER READING

Beshore, George. *Science in Ancient China*. New York: Franklin Watts, Inc. 1998.

Burrell, Roy, and Peter Connolly. *Oxford First Ancient History*. Oxford: Oxford University Press, 1997.

Caselli, Giovanni. *In Search of Pompeii*. New York: Peter Bedrick Books, 1999.

Connolly, Peter. *Pompeii*. Oxford: Oxford University Press Children's Books, 1994.

Gonen, Rivka. *Fired Up! Making Pottery in Ancient Times*. Minneapolis, Minnesota: Runestone Press, 1993.

Hansen, Joyce, and Gary McGowan. *Breaking Ground, Breaking Silence: The Story of New York's African Burial Ground*. New York: Henry Holt & Company, 1998.

Hartz, Paula. *Native American Religions*. New York: Facts on File, Inc., 1997.

Hinds, Kathryn. *The Ancient Romans*. New York: Benchmark Books, 1996.

James, Simon. *Ancient Rome*. New York: Viking Children's Books, 1992.

MacDonald, Fiona, and David Salariya. *First Facts about the Ancient Romans*. New York: Peter Bedrick Books, 1996.

Martell, Hazel Mary, Mark Bergin, David Salariya. *Roman Town*. New York: Franklin Watts, Inc., 1998.

Moss, Carol. *Science in Ancient Mesopotamia*. New York: Franklin Watts, Inc., 1998.

Newton, Douglas. *Seafarers of the Pacific*. Cleveland, Ohio: World Publishing Company, 1964.

Richards, Roy. *Ships through Time*. Austin, Texas: Raintree/Steck Vaughn, 1996.

Odijk, Pamela. *The Phoenicians*. Englewood Cliffs, New Jersey: Silver Burdett Press, 1989.

Rice, Christopher, and Melanie Rice. *The Day a City Was Buried*. New York: DK Publishing, 1998.

Ridington, Jillian, Robin Ridington, and Ian Bateson. *People of the Longhouse*. Buffalo, New York: Firefly Books, 1995.

Stewart, Melissa. *Science in Ancient India*. New York: Franklin Watts, Inc., 1999.

Swentzell, Rina, and Bill Steen. *Children of Clay: A Family of Pueblo Potters*. Minneapolis, Minnesota: Lerner Publications Company, 1992.

SET INDEX

Numbers in **bold type** are volume numbers.

Page numbers in *italics* refer to picture captions or a caption and text reference on the same page.